God's Answer to Anxiety

God's Answer to Anxiety

B. W. Woods

BROADMAN PRESS
Nashville, Tennessee

To my wife, Ann

CONTENTS

1

Elusive Peace

Romans 5:1

Is there any possibility of achieving peace of mind in this world in which we live? The ancient Jeremiah denounced as false prophets those who offered an easy peace when in reality there was no such thing (6:14). The same prophet, despairing of humanity, longed for a little cabin in the wilderness, away from people whose selfishness had made a rat race of life (9:2-5).

Our culture, with its fevered, radioactive brow, faces the chill shadows of the mushroom cloud, and amid the wheezing of an atomic death rattle looks at its offspring only to behold complete moral and spiritual decay—homes breaking up, crime increasing, delinquency growing, addiction to drugs and alcohol escalating, and mental illness at an all-time high. Peace of mind seems long ago and far away.

What is really wrong? I daresay everyone has asked this question more than once. We see people all about us ruining their lives and destroying their families and complaining about the emptiness of life. The basic problems of life do not change. Centuries ago the prophet Jeremiah saw men digging cisterns to store up muddy runoff water while ignoring God's pure spring water (2:13); he saw men becoming barren thistles in the garden of God and degenerating to the level of beasts, driven by animal passions (v. 21); he saw people forgetting the one person who could give life any meaning—God

7

—which is as unbelievable as a bride forgetting her wedding dress (v. 32); and he saw men refusing to walk in the old and respected paths of dignity and decency (6:16).

Jeremiah, too, asked, "What's wrong, anyway?" However, Jeremiah, unlike most bemoaners, knew what was wrong: "No man repented him of his wickedness, saying, What have I done?" (8:6).

There have always been those who take the idea of personal sin lightly. They seek to eradicate it by laughing it off in the name of a more civilized enlightenment. Jeremiah said of such people: "They have healed the hurt of the daughter of my people slightly, saying, Peace, peace; when there is no peace" (v. 11). Jeremiah's diagnosis was that merely ignoring sin is a poor treatment for such a serious malady. Peace does not come so easily. The worn-out cliche, "Everything's going to be all right," has been the insipid iodine applied by multitudes to the cancer of sin. The Bible affirms that nothing is going to be all right as long as man is living apart from God. Since the region of Gilead was noted for its balsam, having medicinal qualities, he asked, "Is there no balm in Gilead; is there no physician there?" (v. 22).

Jeremiah was trying to pinpoint the only alternative to sick living. He was saying that there is a cure for those who will admit their spiritual malady. Jesus himself said, "They that be whole [consider themselves whole] need not [have no use for] a physician, but they that are sick. . . . I am not come to call the righteous [those who are righteous in their own eyes], but sinners to repentance" (Matt. 9:12–13).

The good news of the gospel is that there is a spiritual balm which provides purity for the defiled imagination, strength for the weakened will, and peace for the guilty conscience.

"What have I done?" is an embarrassing review when honestly asked. No one enjoys going over the books when bankruptcy is stamped on every page. Applying a spiritual electrocardiogram may be painful to the ego, but it is the first step toward averting a coronary of the soul.

Everyone advocates a desire for peace. But some have a peculiar way of seeking it. G. W. Johnson commented on Theodore Roosevelt's devotion to peace by saying, "Mr. Roosevelt is always in favor of peace, provided it does not interfere with the fighting." Lord Melbourne is reported to have said that he respected religion, provided it did not interfere with his private life. Many of us are described in these lines:

> We would rather be ruined than changed,
> We would rather die in our dread
> Than climb the cross of the moment
> And let our illusions die.[1]

Such an attitude makes peace of mind a will-o'-the-wisp. Yet the elusiveness of peace makes it all the more desirable. As a result of this void, a number of "peace-of-mind" cults have flourished. Most of them have resembled some type of pseudo-religious hocus-pocus. Peace of mind is presented as obtainable by rising each day with a positive outlook, memorizing a verse of Scripture, thinking good thoughts, and refusing to be discouraged. We are indebted to such advice for reminding us that one's outlook is vitally important. This approach, however, makes peace of mind the product of the mind seeking peace. It all happens within the individual. This comes very close to the position of Christian Science, which denies all evil and speaks of suffering as being "only in the mind."

The Bible affirms the possibility of peace of mind. "Being therefore justified by faith, let us enjoy peace with God" (Rom. 5:1).[2] But the price is high.

Be certain of one thing. Any sign which points to a direct road to peace of mind is deceptive. This is why the manifold programs of self-development always fail to bring peace.

An illustration of this is found in the account of Jesus'

interview with a certain rich young man who had a good program of self-development. The young man had made a habit of keeping the Commandments of God. Yet he felt an emptiness—a lack. During the course of the interview it became evident that the young man's goodness was selfish. His ultimate allegiance was not to goodness, nor to God, but to money and possessions. Since there had to be a showdown, God came out second best. The young man went away clutching his possessions to an empty heart. His program of self-development had not brought peace. Basically it was a negative program. He was assuming that goodness was the absence of misconduct. Findley Edge gives the following illustration: A mother leaves her little boy at home with the oft-repeated warning: "Johnny, be good while I'm gone." What she really means is, "Don't be bad." She wants him not to pull his sister's hair, nor break a window with his bat. When she returns and asks, "Have you been good?" he answers, "Yes, Mother." Neither understands the meaning of goodness. She does not mean to be asking if he has been kind or helpful in a positive way. Johnny may have been asleep all the time she was gone. What she fails to see is that if he has not been bad, he just hasn't been bad. It does not at all mean that he has been good.[3]

However, whether positive or negative, all self-improvement programs fail because they are built around the self. It's a matter of the blind leading the blind.

Peace with God

Peace of mind is not something you cleverly stalk and capture. In this sense it resembles humility. The man who sets out to be humble will most certainly fail. Peace of mind is a side result of other things. There are three prerequisites for enjoying peace of mind. The first hurdle is to be at peace with God. This is what is involved in being "justified by faith." Peace implies the cessation of hostilities.

I shall never forget the day news came that World War II had ended. My family drove from our farm into the nearby county seat. The stores were all closed. Cars, honking wildly, were whizzing up and down Main Street. Firecrackers were popping everywhere. Flags were waving. Why all the celebration? A horrible war was over. Hostilities had ceased. Life could pick up the pieces and begin all over. It was time to be joyful, but it cannot even be compared to the inward joy of peace with God!

To some extent, every person relives the experience of the prodigal son who ran away from home and from the loving care of his father only to find that real joy was found in returning and finding forgiveness and acceptance. The Bible affirms that men are "by nature the children of wrath" (Eph. 2:3). You are engaged in rebellion against God if you reject his will, his grace, and his love—if you choose to "go it alone." For this reason the apostle John defines sin as unbelief (John 3:18). Basic to the concept of faith is the idea of commitment to the lordship of Christ. This means an unconditional surrender. Until such capitulation occurs, you remain in unbelief. You remain uncommitted. This leaves you with guilt on your hands. There can be no peace of mind until guilt is removed. Most peace-of-mind programs overlook this basic problem.

How do you get guilt off your hands? Multitudes have tried psychoanalysis; but O. Hobart Mowrer, research professor of psychology at the University of Illinois, argues that this is a blind alley. Psychoanalysis assumes (from Freud) that guilt is not real and tries to effect a cure by convincing the "patient" that he is not guilty. Mowrer affirms that guilt is real and is the source of mental illness.[4] Concerning psychoanalysis, Mowrer writes, "Despite some pretentious affirmations to the contrary, the fact is that psychoanalysis, on which modern 'dynamic' psychiatry is largely based, is in a state of virtual collapse and imminent demise."[5] Mowrer continues, "People do not merely 'talk' themselves into sin; they *act*. And by the same token, I do not believe anyone ever talks himself out of sin. Again there must be action, and this action must involve not only confession, of an ultimately open type, but also 'atonement.' " [6]

Guilt demands payment and restitution. But how can you make things right? The whole point is that you can't. Only God, the one wronged, can remove your guilt and effect reconciliation. Christ died to pay the price your guilt demands —to suffer for your sins. Thus it is possible for you to be "reconciled to God by the death of his Son" (Rom. 5:10). You can be declared not guilty through a faith surrender to Christ. Justification is a legal term meaning to be declared "not guilty." This is to be "justified by faith."

Peace with God is a relationship with God, not a state of mind. It is a relationship that affects your state of mind. Peace of mind can never be captured by onslaught. It must come as a by-product of being at peace with God.

Reaction to Problems

Enjoying this peace daily is a matter of our daily relation to the will of God. As a young pastor I used to be puzzled when negligent Christians became "touchy" toward me. Then I discovered the truth: when one is not at peace with God, and his will, one has no peace of mind. He cannot "*enjoy* peace with God." He is touchy with everyone who reminds him of his relationship to God.

But the truth of the matter is that one can have made peace with God through a faith surrender to Christ and yet not have peace of mind. Although faith ushers us into the harbor of God's grace (Rom. 5:2), we will not have peace of mind unless we learn how to regard the pressures of life. The apostle Paul says, "We glory in tribulations" (v. 3). He speaks of the afflictions and pressures of life which bear down daily.

These problems come in various guises: hardships, reverses, abuses, unbearable burdens. Being at peace with God enables us to look on such pressures in a different light—to remain confident in the midst of them. Paul tells us why: "Knowing that tribulation worketh patience; and patience, experience; and experience, hope" (vv. 3–4). These words present a vivid picture of a skilled craftsman who, with tools in hand, hammers out of the raw material the finished product. Pressures hammer out in our character the patience to endure. This is the power to carry on, to keep going, to plod ahead.

The tools are then handed to Endurance which begins to hammer out in our character experience. "Experience" literally means to have been put through the test and found sufficient. It was a word used to speak of metal from which the dross had been removed. It is the word used to set forth the qualifications of a deacon, "Let these also first be *proved*" (1 Tim. 3:10). Such men must have passed through the fire of testing.

Now you can see why Paul encourages us to "glory in tribulations." The pressures of life can strengthen character and produce a genuine hope.

Christian Hope

This leads to the third prerequisite for peace of mind: learning to hope in what will never disappoint. Paul continues, "Hope maketh not ashamed" (Rom. 5:5). You don't have to take your stand with those who see their hopes dashed upon the rocks of time. Count on men and they will fail you. Trust in riches and they will desert you in those dark hours of grief. It is possible to have hope which can never bring shame or loss. Christian hope is directed, rejoicingly, toward the glory of God, into whose image we shall someday be transformed. Christian hope is toward "eternal life, which God, [who] cannot lie, promised before the world began" (Titus 1:2).

Genuine hope is not possible for you, apart from faith in Christ. If you choose to be self-sufficient, self-righteous, and self-sustaining, then you, like the lowly spider, have chosen to risk all on a flimsy, self-spun web. In contrast, Christian hope is an anchor to the soul, sure and steadfast.

You ask me for proof of the security of Christian hope? My answer is twofold: God's love already exhibited by Christ's death, and the power manifested by Christ's living presence. God's love has already been exhibited, for "God commendeth his love toward us, in that, while we were yet sinners, Christ died for us" (Rom. 5:8). If God loved rebellious men enough to allow Christ to die for them, then how *much more* does God love those surrendering to Christ in faith? Romans 5:9 reminds us, "Much more then, being now justified by his blood, we shall be saved from wrath through him."

Christian hope involves not only eternity but also life in the here and now. What hope is there for strength and victory in this life? The answer is found in the powerful presence of the risen Lord. "If, when we were enemies, we were reconciled to God by the death of his Son, much more, being reconciled, we shall be saved by his life" (Rom. 5:10). In every way the Christian has *much more*.

The death of Christ made salvation of your soul possible, but salvation involves a present victory as well. Suppose an alcoholic is converted. The next morning he faces the world with the peace of God in his heart. Yet he still has a problem. He is still an alcoholic. His body is still tormented by a physical craving. Christ's death made forgiveness of his sins possible, but who is to deliver him from this demonic thirst? The dynamic presence of the risen Christ. This is what it means to be "saved by his life." This is the bonus; this is the *much more!* You don't face life alone. The living Christ is with you every moment. His promise is: "There hath no temptation taken you but such as is common to man: but God is faithful, who will not suffer you to be tempted above that ye are able; but will with the temptation also make a way to escape, that ye may be able to bear it" (1 Cor. 10:13).

Paul echoes this by saying, "I am crucified with Christ: nevertheless I live; yet not I, but Christ liveth in me" (Gal. 2:20). Peace of mind is not so elusive after all. It is possible for all. It comes from being at peace with God through faith in Jesus Christ. Faith is surrender, unconditionally. Peace of mind involves "enjoying" this peace with God. It requires a proper attitude toward pressures and the placing of your hope in what will never disappoint.

Now for a personal question: "Do you want such peace?" Perhaps a more appropriate question would be: "Do you dare to have such peace?" A faith-surrender means taking a chance. It's like buying a pair of shoes without being able to try them on first. The promise of Jesus is: "If anyone is willing to keep on doing God's will, he will know whether my teaching comes from God, or merely expresses my own ideas" (John 7:17, Williams).

Has the time come for you to decide? The Bible is full of admonitions to do just that. Moses cried, "Who is on the Lord's side?" (Ex. 32:26). Joshua's challenge was: "Choose you this day whom ye will serve" (24:15).

A medical student can study all his life but he will never learn surgery until he takes the scalpel in hand. Most of the people who heard Jesus during his earthly life were content to make of that great experience nothing more than an argument over religion. They wrangled over who he was and what he did. They missed the opportunity to respond to his personal invitation to try it his way—to surrender to his lordship and see for themselves whether or not he had the answer to life's deepest needs. Jesus still offers peace to those who are weary of strife. But let me make one thing clear. Peace is not the absence of all conflicts. The Christian life is a constant struggle.

2

The Struggle for Victory

Romans 7:21–23

Do you mean everything is not settled once Christ is accepted as Saviour? That is exactly what I mean. The Bible is very plain about this. The apostle Paul reminds the Christians at Rome that they, through faith in Christ, are dead with regard to sin and alive with regard to God. Yet in the same breath, he admonishes them to stop letting sin lord it over them (Rom. 6:11–12). Paul is pointing out the fact that dying to sin begins at conversion but requires a lifetime for ultimate completion. You are a new person after conversion: "If any man be in Christ, he is a new creature: old things are passed away; behold, all things are become new" (2 Cor. 5:17). But it is with great struggle that the "old things" and the "old man" are cast aside. The process involved is that of progress in the Christian life. The new Christian is still a babe where spiritual matters are concerned. Growing up is always a battle. Failure to understand this causes many Christians to despair as they experience this inner conflict.

H. G. Wells said of his character, Mr. Polly, that "he was a walking civil war." This well describes the inner warfare which belongs to the Christian who seeks to grow spiritually.

Romans 7 is Paul's autobiographical account of his own inner warfare. Because Paul was so mightily used of God, we have a tendency to deify him. In Romans 7, this great apostle lays bare his own heart and his own feeling of weakness. His personal testimony stands as a word of encouragement to others who are experiencing the same struggle.

16

Paul's autobiographical section is divided into two parts: Romans 7:7–13 presents his preconversion experiences by way of reminiscence; the remainder of the chapter presents his struggle after conversion. This division is supported by the use of past tense verbs in Romans 7:7–13, followed by a shift to present tense verbs beginning with Romans 7:14, wherein Paul states the problem which faces every Christian from the moment of conversion: "For we know that the law is spiritual, but I am made of flesh that is frail" (7:14, Williams). The Christian is still human and open to temptation.

Background of the Struggle

Since the preconversion experience is the backdrop for the Christian struggle for progress, let us examine it as found in Paul's testimony. As the apostle Paul looks back, he is aware of having been deceived by sin. His story goes back to the time of his childhood—before the age of accountability in spiritual matters. He says of this time, "I was once alive when I had no connection with the law, but when the command came, sin revived, and then I died" (Rom. 7:9, Williams). This is another way of saying that a person is not responsible for his sin until he reaches an age at which he understands the meaning of God's laws. At such a time, sin becomes real and brings spiritual death through transgression of God's laws.

Sin (Satan, the tempter, is here almost personified, as "sin" is used with the definite article the) takes advantage of the opportunity: "Sin, taking occasion by the commandment [of God], wrought in me all manner of concupiscence [lust]. For without the law sin was dead" (Rom. 7:8). The word translated "occasion" is a military term referring to a beachhead—a base of operations. Satan used the commandments of God as a base of operations to assail Paul with temptations. Hear Paul again as he says, "I had not known lust, except the law had said, Thou shalt not covet" (Rom. 7:7).

Sinful human nature being what it is, we desire that which is forbidden. In his *Confessions,* Augustine tells of his own weakness in this area:

I lusted to thieve, and did it, compelled by no hunger, nor poverty. . . . For I stole that, of which I had enough, and much better . . . but joyed in the theft and sin itself. A pear tree there was near our vineyard. . . . To shake and rob this, some lewd young fellows of us went . . . and took huge loads, not for our eating, but to fling to the very hogs, having only tasted them. And this, but to do what we liked only, because it was misliked.

Satan deceives us and thus perverts the purpose of God's law, which was given to mark off for us the good life: "The commandment, which was ordained to life, I found to be unto death. For sin, taking occasion by the commandment, deceived me, and by it slew me" (Rom. 7:10–11).

Satan leads a man on until his neck is through the noose of God's law and he finds himself a transgressor, living under the penalty of death—spiritual death. Romans 7:11 says, "Sin seduced me" (Barclay), or, "Sin completely made me lose my way" (Robertson).

As Paul shares his own experience, we see how it (and our own) parallels that of the first man, Adam. Satan's deceit is our downfall. He says we can sin and not die, sow and not reap.

However, Paul is anxious to keep the record straight concerning God's law. "The law is holy, and the commandment holy, and just, and good" (Rom. 7:12). The law merely defines sin, as an X-ray photograph reveals the presence of an inner malignancy. God's purpose was not for his law to bring a man to spiritual death. The law was given to reveal sin to us as the terrible monstrosity it is (cf. Rom. 7:13).

The Problem

Paul often told of his own conversion on the dusty Damascus road and how he suddenly realized his life was an open rebellion against Christ. From that moment Paul was a different person. Yet he shares with us the problem—still "made of flesh." This is the reason conversion is often referred to as a beginning—not an end. The Christian finds himself still "in the flesh" but admonished not to live "according to the flesh" (Rom. 8:12–13). There is a difference. The Christian still lives in the fleshly body, with its weaknesses. He has a new nature but finds that the remnants of his old nature are still with him. These remnants were once the slave of sin. The flesh can still be tempted. It can still serve as a beachhead for Satan's forays. The old nature has been put to death but refuses to stop breathing and die. This accounts for the struggle for Christian growth. Paul admits that although he wants to do right, he sometimes fails: "Now then it is no more I that do it, but sin that dwelleth in me" (Rom. 7:17). Paul is not excusing himself from guilt; he is pointing out the problem.

At conversion, the Monster is cast out and Christ is made the center of life. Yet the Usurper loiters on the outskirts, awaiting his opportunity. He takes up squatter's rights out on the fringes of life and hangs on. To overlook this threat is to find defeat in the Christian life. Paul explains this to the church at Corinth also: "I keep under my body, and bring it into subjection: lest that by any means, when I have preached to others, I myself should be a castaway" (1 Cor. 9:27). Paul is not discussing the possibility of losing salvation but the possibility of disqualifying himself in some moment of weakness so that God would have to use someone else and let him sit on the shelf.

The warfare involved in Christian growth is not marked by continual intensity but is rather sporadic. Major battles loom up from time to time. You will find yourself saying with Paul, "To will is present with me; but *how* to perform that which is good I find not. For the good that I would I do not: but the evil which I would not, that I do" (Rom. 7:18–19).

There will be times when you find yourself practicing evil in spite of your good intentions. At such times you will echo Paul: "I delight in the law of God after the inward man: but I see another law in my members, warring against the law of my mind, and bringing me into captivity to the law of sin which is in my members" (Rom. 7:22-23).

Paul admits there were times when he applauded God's law and yet fell victim to Satan's full scale attack so that momentarily sin was his captor. Somehow, it is an encouragement to know that a great Christian like Paul cried, "O wretched man that I am [literally, 'wretched man I']! who shall deliver me from the body of this death?" (Rom. 7:24). There were times when Paul was so aware of the frailty of his own strength as a new man in Christ, and so aware of the strength of the old nature which refused to die, that he wondered how he could ever have the victory over temptations that he desired. His cry is like that of a radiologist who finds a malignant shadow on his own X ray. It is not enough to know what's right. You can memorize instructions on how to hit a golf ball, but hitting it properly is another matter.

The "body of death" Paul refers to may well be an allusion to the ancient custom of chaining a criminal to the corpse of the man he murdered, making him drag the decaying body about until his own living body absorbed the poison and succumbed. At any rate, Paul is speaking of the "old man" he once was who keeps hanging on. Phillips translates: "It is an agonizing situation, and who on earth can set me free from the clutches of my own sinful nature?"

Assurance of Victory

The example of the converted alcoholic, mentioned in the previous chapter, applies here. Forgiveness of his sins came in the moment of conversion, but victory over his demonic craving came through a daily struggle. Deliverance can come only through the power of the present, living Christ. This is the answer Paul gives to his own question: "Who shall deliver me . . . ? I thank God through Jesus Christ our Lord" (Rom. 7:24-25).

By this time you may be wondering how there can be any peace of mind in the midst of such warfare for Christian victory. There can be—through Christ. Paul found the secret in the fact that he was not dependent on his own strength. The living Christ gives assurance of victory. What can't be done by conscience, law, or human strength is accomplished in Christ. We can expect deliverance and victory.

Strangely enough, many Christians who accept salvation by faith try to attain Christian growth by themselves. The secret to peace amidst struggle is to be found in a daily self-surrender to Christ. E. Stanley Jones, the noted missionary, relates the following example of such self-surrender: "A young man came to our Ashram and in the 'Overflowing Heart' said: 'I've resigned as the general manager of the universe.' The surrender of the self had cut him down to size and had cut his job down to size—something that God and he could manage together." [1]

John Stuart Mill's commentary on his own stern education was, "I had a rudder, but no sail." The possibility of a "sail" to go with the "rudder" is expressed in an old Sunday School song:

> I feel the winds of God today,
> Today my sail I lift.

There have been many dramatic stories of escape from the terrors of Communist-held East Germany. But none equals the relief experienced when you stop trying to do everything in your own strength—when you escape self-deliverance and find the joy of God-deliverance.

The psalmist declares, "God is our refuge and strength, a

very present help in trouble" (46:1). The occasion which
called forth these words is one of the most dramatic events in
the Old Testament. During the reign of King Hezekiah the
Syrian general, Sennacherib, approached Jerusalem with a
mighty army of 185,000 men. Sennacherib sent an insulting
message to Hezekiah, demanding surrender and scoffing at the
power of Hezekiah's God. Well aware of his inability to de-
fend his city against Sennacherib, Hezekiah went into the
Temple and prayerfully asked a solution from God. God answered through the person of the prophet Isaiah, saying, "Jerusalem shall be delivered." During the darkness of night God
scattered and destroyed the massive Syrian army. Out of this
experience the inspired psalmist affirms, "God is our refuge
and strength, a very present help in trouble." His advice to us
who are so prone to face our problems with a frenzied and
noisome search for a solution is, "Be still, and know that I am
God" (46:10). This advice is much more helpful than: "When
uncertain, when in doubt, run in circles, scream and shout."

Few of us will ever face seas of opposition or turmoil of soul
like those confronting Martin Luther during the Reformation.
Yet we are inspired in our own struggles by the words of one
of his great hymns: "A mighty fortress is our God, a bulwark
never failing."

In the face of insurmountable odds the prophet Elisha once
stated, "Fear not: for they that be with us are more than they
that be with them" (2 Kings 6:16). With eyes of faith he had
seen that the surrounding hillsides were filled with the hosts
of God. As James Russell Lowell put it in "The Present Crisis":

Though the cause of Evil prosper, yet 'tis truth alone is strong,
. . . .
Truth forever on the scaffold, Wrong forever on the throne,—
Yet that scaffold sways the future, and, behind the dim unknown,
Standeth God within the shadow, keeping watch above his own.

Hear this promise to Christians: "There hath no temptation taken you but such as is common to man: but God is faithful, who will not suffer you to be tempted above that ye are able; but will with the temptation also make a way to escape, that ye may be able to bear it" (1 Cor. 10:13).

The Christ who was able to break sin's grip on us by his death is able to give us daily victory over its deceitful efforts by his life. If man can't save himself, neither can he, once saved, effect Christian growth by himself. Paul discovered this great truth in his own life. He exclaimed, "Now then, there is no judgment against them who are in Christ Jesus . . . because what the law could not possibly do, since it was dependent on fleshly strength, God did in sending his own Son as a man, and as a sacrifice for sin, to defeat sin personally" (Rom. 8:1–3, translation mine).

"Now then" is temporal. It has in it the sigh of relief. Like the frantic alpine climber who sees his rope slipping and at the moment of greatest panic feels a solid ledge beneath his feet where he thought there was only a death fall, so Paul wipes the perspiration from his brow as he realizes the hand of God is always there to hold him up and carry him along.

All the law could ever do was condemn sin on paper. It is another matter to defeat sin in the flesh, personally. Civil laws forbid murder, but the murderer is defeated only when the policeman personally subdues him.

Christ wrought this victory "that the righteousness intended by the giving of the law might be brought to fulness in us who do not walk in human strength, but who walk in the strength of God's Spirit" (Rom. 8:4, translation mine). Paul concludes, "To be spiritually minded is life and peace" (v. 6).

Before you become discouraged in your attempt to grow spiritually, remember that there is a certain assurance which the Christian warfare provides. The people who should worry are those who have no struggle. No struggle usually means no purpose—no salvation. A corpse no longer struggles for breath. A wrestler who ceases to struggle has surrendered.

The only alternative to struggle is defeat. Many years after penning the Roman letter, the aged apostle Paul warns a young preacher named Timothy about this alternative. He speaks of the danger of making a shipwreck of faith—of faith on the rocks (1 Tim. 1:19). Paul knew all about shipwrecks, for he had experienced three. He had seen the dismal sight of a floundering wreckage lying helpless while relentless waves broke over it and the roar of the sea sounded its death dirge. A shipwreck is a vivid metaphor of abandoned hopes and frustrated ambitions. Yet the saddest of all wrecks is the shipwreck of faith—faith which has welled up in the breast and dreamed of great ventures. The church was still in its infancy but already its shores were littered with wrecks that once were vibrant souls thrilled with the prospect of life's voyage. It might be well for us to listen to Paul's word about the shipwreck of faith: "This charge I commit unto thee, son Timothy . . . that thou . . . mightest war a good warfare; holding faith, and a good conscience; which some having put away concerning faith have made shipwreck: of whom is Hymenaeus and Alexander; whom I have delivered unto Satan, that they may learn not to blaspheme" (1 Tim. 1:18-20).

Keep in mind that when Paul speaks of the shipwreck of faith he is equating faith with the Christian life—the life of commitment. It is possible to make a wreck of your Christian life, but only by giving up. No one ever wrecks his life until he quits trying. A poor memory causes many people to throw in the towel. It is said that John Newton, who sailed the seas as a slave trader before his conversion and call to preach, kept a placard above his mantle: "Thou shalt remember that thou wast a bondman in the land of Egypt, and the Lord thy God redeemed thee" (Deut. 15:15).

Paul mentions two men, Hymenaeus and Alexander, who have ceased their Christian struggle and cast overboard their Christian calling and conscience. Any time you see the wreckage of a Christian's life you can be sure it was self-inflicted by a careless course of conduct and a purposeful disregard of Christian conscience. The Christian's warfare is not one short battle after which one may discard his weapons. It is an extended struggle. It is not a fifty-yard dash but a thousand-mile marathon.

Good conscience comes by practicing what one preaches. To do otherwise is to cast conscience overboard. This is like tossing a ship's ballast over the side. The ship becomes unmanageable and is easily driven and tossed by every wind. Every church I have ever known has its "Roll of the Shipwrecked." A good conscience is the most rewarding treasure and the noblest heritage to be found. It is priceless because money can't buy it, the covetous cannot steal it, and hardship cannot harm it. Only self-disregard of it can denude it of its crown.

Paul equates making a wreckage of one's Christian life with the sin of blasphemy. It is the failure to live what one professes. Paul says he has delivered Hymenaeus and Alexander to Satan "that they may learn not to blaspheme." Paul is saying he has cast them out of the Christian fellowship as a disciplinary punishment. To a genuine Christian this is punishment indeed.

One of the rewards an ancient Spartan received when he won in the Olympic games was the privilege of standing beside his king in battle. Plutarch tells of a Spartan wrestler who refused a considerable bribe and with great struggle won his match. Someone who knew about the proposed bribe chided the wrestler by asking what he would get out of his expensive victory. The Spartan answered, "The honor of standing in front of my king in battle." His reward was to serve and if need be to die for his king.

The world is probably trying to bribe you even now. Do bargain sales get your tithe? Does Sunday television get your time instead of God? Do dog-eat-dog practices offer you greater reward than the joy of a clear conscience? Many a beautiful vessel has set out in full sail to follow a divinely marked course only to be washed up on an alien shore with shattered prow and broken masts. The helmsman, tired of watching the compass and battling the elements, went below to sleep. He gave up the struggle. He gave up because he misunderstood the reason for it and the reward of it. Thank God for your struggle and for his promise of your final victory.

This word of caution, however. As you struggle for progress in the Christian life, you will sooner or later be confronted with tragedies and suffering. You will find yourself without any meaningful explanations unless you have some grasp of God's great, eternal purpose. The next chapter should prove helpful at this point.

3

Understanding God's Purpose

Romans 8:28

"We know that God is able to bring good out of any circumstance in the lives of those who love him" (Rom. 8:28).[1]

No one can deny the complexity of life. Only a fool would claim to have the answer to everything that happens. Yet the apostle Paul, facing the same winds of adversity and forces of evil which are with us today, confidently asserts, "I reckon that the sufferings of this present time are not worthy to be compared with the glory which shall be revealed in us" (Rom. 8:18). "Reckon" is a bookkeeping term. Paul says he has added up all the columns, has taken everything into consideration, and is certain that Christianity has more to offer than any other way of life. The rewards of eternity far outweigh the hardships of the present. Paul is dogmatic at this point because he has discovered the great, unchanging purpose of God which operates regardless of what the future holds. God is all-powerful and "is able to bring good out of any circumstance in the lives of those who love him, those who in accordance to his purpose have accepted his call." To understand this wonderful promise requires a biblical definition of "good."

God's Purpose: Hope Amidst Anxious Futility

The Bible is open and honest. The inspired apostle freely admits that life is surrounded by futility: "We know that the

27

whole creation groaneth and travaileth in pain together until
now. And not only they, but ourselves also, which have the
firstfruits of the Spirit, even we ourselves groan within ourselves, waiting for the adoption, to wit, the redemption of our
body" (Rom. 8:22–23).

Nature is here personified and shown to be restless and
unfulfilled. Nature, as well as man, was affected by Adam's
fall. Everywhere we see evidence of death and decay. The
fury of the elements, the catastrophes of nature, the scourge of
barrenness—all are but the groanings of a fallen world. The
present world never reaches perfection and always disap-
points our expectations. Nature yearns for fulfilment promised
in the new heaven and the new earth (Rev. 21:1).

In a lecture on revelation, Schelling once said: "Nature,
with its melancholy charm, resembles a bride who, at the very
moment when she was fully attired for marriage, saw the
bridegroom to whom she was to be united die on the very day
fixed for the marriage. She still stands with her fresh crown
and in her bridal dress, but her eyes are full of tears." [2]

Man in general shares something of nature's emptiness.
Even Christians yearn for the time of ultimate fulfilment:
"And not only they, but ourselves also, which have the first-
fruits of the Spirit, even we ourselves groan within ourselves,
waiting for the adoption, to wit, the redemption of our body"
(Rom. 8:23).

Since the coming resurrection which will usher in eternity
also involves a new heaven and a new earth, all of creation
breathlessly waits. Phillips translates Romans 8:19–21: "The
whole creation is on tiptoe to see the wonderful sight of the
sons of God coming into their own. The world of creation
cannot as yet see reality, not because it chooses to be blind,
but because in God's purpose it has been so limited—yet it has
been given hope. And the hope is that in the end the whole of
created life will be rescued from the tyranny of change and

decay, and have its share in that magnificent liberty which can only belong to the children of God!" [3]

In the midst of universal groaning and futility, the Christian finds hope in the knowledge that God is daily working out his purpose. This Christian hope delivers us from the despair surrounding us: "We were saved by this hope, but in our moments of impatience let us remember that hope always means waiting for something that we do not yet possess. But if we hope for something we cannot see, then we must settle down to wait for it in patience" (Rom. 8:24–25, Phillips).

The element of hope is an important and exciting part of the Christian faith. We do not yet have all we are to receive. Luccock observes: " 'Above this darksome circus shine the stars.' There is always a tragedy about the words 'paid in full.' When all the profit of life is paid immediately, there is a dreary finality about it. No mysterious remainders of life, no glory of tomorrow to look forward to; the whole thing is receipted. There it is, 'paid in full.' The high adventure of life is over." [4]

Let the worldling settle for what this earthly life can offer; the Christian has wisely refused to sell out so cheaply. God's unchanging purpose guarantees the reality of our hope.

God's Purpose Not Always Clear

This is not to say that because we are Christians we will always be able to ascertain the working out of God's purpose.

Job is a prime illustration. He lost all his children and possessions. The Scriptures tell us that God allowed Satan to afflict Job in order to prove the reality of Job's faith. God wanted to show Satan, and the world, that Job would be faithful, whether rich or poor; whether surrounded by sons and daughters; or sitting alone in an empty house of memories. But Job never did know what God's purpose was! At first Job searched for some explanation for his sufferings, but no explanation came. His questions were never answered. They were rather removed by a deepened awareness of God's presence amidst his suffering. Job announces the end of his querulous pilgrimage: "I have heard of thee by the hearing of the ear: but now mine eye seeth thee. Wherefore I abhor myself, and repent in dust and ashes" (42:5–6). Although God's purpose was never clear, Job learned to submit to it in simple trust.

There are times when "we know not what we should pray for" (Rom. 8:26). In our human weakness, clouded by sin, beset by discouragement and selfishness, we often mistake God's workings, or fail to see them altogether. When every road is a dead end and no answer seems right, we feel the need of prayer and experience the frustration of not knowing that for which we should pray. At such moments, "the Spirit also helpeth our infirmities . . . [and] maketh intercession for us with groanings which cannot be uttered" (v. 26). The word translated "helpeth" literally means "to take hold on the other side." When our load of frustration becomes heavy, the Holy Spirit takes hold with us. The picture is that of a child struggling with a heavy bucket of water. He suddenly feels the load lifted because his father has taken hold on the opposite side.

Many times have I stood with a grief-stricken family by the bedside of a loved one whose body was racked in the agonizing throes of an incurable malignancy, feeling the need of prayer and not knowing what to ask for—whether the prolonging of life or the sudden coming of death. At such times the deepest and most meaningful prayer may be the unuttered agony of a heart, reaching out for God in complete helplessness and selflessness. No words seem right; yet you feel the deep necessity of communing with God. It is then that God's Spirit within us bears witness with our spirit, and whether or not the words uttered have meaning, there is communion with

God. Sometimes words are insufficient to express our feelings. Paul speaks of such an experience he once had (2 Cor. 12:4).

In moments like these, though we cannot grasp God's purpose, we know it is unchangeable and can be trusted. If a wife does not trust her husband out of her sight she doesn't trust him. The test of our trust is not when God's working is easily discernible, but rather when we can't see him for the shadows. Yet, with Lowell, we know he is there:

Truth forever on the scaffold, Wrong forever on the throne,—
Yet that scaffold sways the future, and, behind the dim unknown,
Standeth God within the shadow, keeping watch above his own.

God's Purpose: Glorification of His Elect

What then is God's unchanging purpose that works amidst anxious futility and in ways we cannot often fathom? The time has come for a definition of the "good." The world equates "good" with luxury, ease, and material prosperity. The correct definition of the "good" mentioned in Romans 8:28 is found in Romans 8:29: "to be conformed to the image of his Son." This is the supreme good toward which God's purpose is moving—to make his children Christlike. In contrast to the universal groaning, stands God's goal already marked off—Christlikeness.

Romans 8:28–29 tells us some important things about life. To begin with, everything doesn't happen because God made it happen. God gives to each person the freedom of choice. You can choose your god and your way of life. You can live carefully or recklessly. Of course God is able to perform miracles and prevent any action he desires, but God performs miracles only for redemptive purposes. God's power is not a checkbook on which you can draw by taking reckless chances and thinking God is obligated to save you from harm.

I shall never forget the Saturday night my phone awakened me and the voice of a church member blurted, "Pastor, there has been a terrible wreck and one of our young people is in the car." I dressed hurriedly and walked briskly through the crisp winter night. The mishap had occurred only two blocks away. The pale moon cast an ominous glow upon the gathering onlookers and revealed in their midst the crinkled mass which had once been a car, now molded around a giant pecan tree beside the boulevard. Several men had fastened a log chain around the doorposts and were trying to pull the collapsed car apart. From somewhere underneath the wreckage came the frantic screams of a boy, cursing deliriously and crying for help. I saw the man who had called me kneeling beside the open car door, and as I approached I made out the limp body of a young girl—the daughter of one of our church members. Her body from the waist down was pinned in the car and from the waist up was being held off the ground by my friend. Her face was a bloody pulp. She was dead. I walked around the car and stumbled over a pile of cans—beer cans. The police counted ninety-seven as they removed the car.

I numbly went to tell a mother her daughter was dead.

Later, I learned the whole story. The girl had chosen to date a boy known for drunkenness. The five young people in the car had chosen to ice down a tub of beer in the trunk of the car. They had then chosen to try to reach a speed of one hundred miles an hour on the city boulevard. You know the rest.

The boy driving the car lived. His parents told him not to worry about the death of the girl because it was just "her time to go." They said the girl would have died that night anyway, even if she had not been in the wreck. They said it was "just God's will"! What those parents told their son was utter blasphemy. Nothing that happened that night was God's will. God never wills that anyone get drunk and drive carelessly.

Yet, out of that tragedy, I saw several Christians made more

Christlike. God did not cause the tragedy, but was able to use it to deepen the spiritual awareness of his children.

We live in a world marked by sin. Disease is a part of this fallen world. Do not think that every time someone has cancer it is because God planted the malignancy himself. The Christian is not promised perfect health. But he is promised the presence of the loving Heavenly Father when disease and death come.

One of my dearest fellow pastors had a four-year-old daughter who suffered a relapse from common measles. The youngster died in a screaming seizure. As I tried to comfort the father, he said, "My wife and I are determined to let this draw us nearer the Lord." God did not purposely take the child. But God was able to use that tragic loss to make those parents more Christlike. Our Lord suffered every agony and is able to use our suffering to make us more like him.

Everything that happens is not good. You cannot say, "Everything is for the best." But you can say, if you are a Christian (for the promise is only to Christians), that God is with you in every situation, and has the power to use every situation for your spiritual good.

A successful businessman, a member of a church I once pastored, suddenly suffered a massive heart attack. For days his life hung in the balance. After he had begun to recover, we had a number of long talks together. During one of these, he said, "Pastor, I haven't been much of a Christian. I've been a better civic leader and lodge member than I have a church member. I've had time to do a lot of thinking, and from now on my church is going to come before any other organization." He continued, "Also, I have an interest in a business which is forced to have a liquor license. I am going to get out of that partnership." His following statement was the clincher. He said, "Pastor, this heart attack is the most wonderful thing that has happened to me in a long time." You see, God's power was operating in the aftermath of a heart attack to help mold this man into the image of Christlikeness.

Although God does not cause everything to happen, and though all that happens is not good, God's power is able to use even the greatest tragedy, as the sculptor uses his chisel, to conform you to the image of his Son. A diamond is not beautiful until cut and polished. Christlikeness requires drastic surgery and is always painful. The sad truth is that many people do not want the good. They want heaven but not holiness.

Notice the promise of purpose is limited to those who have accepted God's call through faith in Christ. To the uncommitted worldling, nothing works together for ultimate good. Success makes him self-sufficient and tragedy makes him bitter. He cannot be made into the image of the Saviour whom he has rejected. All of life is without purpose and is utterly wasted.

Christian assurance, on the other hand, is not dependent on the absence of trials and heartaches. The Christian faces life's trials knowing the final outcome. God is guiding his children toward eternal glory and conforming them into the image of Christ. This is the supreme good. No earthly vicissitude can thwart God's purpose. No wonder Paul could say he had added everything up and found that Christianity had more to offer than any other way of life. We can say it too!

4

God's Hand Amidst Grief

Genesis 37:34–35

The story is told of a gentle, godly man who, having purged his own garden of thistles, felt it his obligation to do the same for his neighbor's garden. But after finishing the job for his neighbor, he saw a whole hillside covered with thistles and began to weep. He suddenly realized he could never cleanse the world of all its thistles. To make matters worse, when he arrived at church the next Sunday morning he found a woman arranging the altar flowers—they were Scotch thistles. Thistles had now invaded even his church.[1]

No man is exempt from grief and deep loss—not even a man of faith. Jacob has played many roles in his lifetime; he has run the gamut all the way from the role of God's enemy to that of God's servant. Yet it is at precisely the moment when he is playing the role of obedient servant that grief caves in upon him. Before we wonder why grief came after he had become obedient rather than while he was a renegade, we need to recognize that it is the servant of God who is best equipped to face his grief. It is fortunate for Jacob that it came not during his rebellious years but during his faithful pilgrimage. When enshrouded in a world of sorrow, what is one to do? How does God fit into the scheme of things when grief descends?

The Grief

The same chapter that records Jacob's great experience of rededication at Bethel also contains the account of two deaths

—the death of his wife Rachel and his father Isaac. However the immediate cause of Jacob's grief is the loss of his favorite son, Joseph. Jacob's world caves in as his older sons bring to him the shredded and torn coat of Joseph. The huge blotches of blood smeared upon the coat proclaim the silent message that Joseph is dead. (Of course you and I know better—we know that the jealous brothers have merely sold Joseph as a slave to some merchantmen heading toward Egypt—but this does not change the grief of the father who believes his son to be dead.)

In this experience we see again the futility of human comforters: "All his sons and all his daughters rose up to comfort him; but he refused to be comforted; and he said, For I will go down into the grave unto my son mourning. Thus his father wept for him" (Gen. 37:35).

When Edmund Burke was prime minister of England his support of the long wars with France was carried on with no thought of the sorrows which those wars brought home to multitudes of hearts. It was not until his own son was killed in battle that the whole world of politics and personal ambition lost their meaning. He wrote, "The storms have gone over me, and I lie like one of those old oaks which the late hurricane has scattered about me. I am stripped of all my honors; I am torn up by the roots and lie prostrate on the earth. I am alone. I have none to meet my enemies in the gate. I live in an inverted order. They who ought to have succeeded me have gone before me. They who should have been to me as posterity are in the place of ancestors." [2]

There is somehow a double sadness when the natural order of loss by death occurs. It is hard enough for a son to give up his father, but, oh, how the loss deepens when a father must give up his son. What father who has experienced such a loss would not freely cry out as did David at his son's death: "O Absalom, my son, would to God that I had died in your place."

The failure of human comforters at least brings to focus the comfort which can be found in God. The answer to Jeremiah's question is an affirmative one: "Yes, there is a balm in Gilead." But it must be applied to the heart by the hand of God. It does not remove the scar; it only heals the wound. God is able to lead Jacob through his valley of grief and show him that he still has things to live for. There is still a purpose for his life as well as that of his family.

God's Hand

As God's consoling hand is laid upon one's back in grief he can either rebel against it in bitterness or he can respond in such a way as to be led through the darkness to the sunlight. God is not the source of Jacob's grief, but God has a way through Jacob's grief and has the power to make even of this grief a blessing. The almighty power of God is never more vividly demonstrated than it is as he takes hold of our sorrows and losses and is able to use them for the fulfilment of his divine purpose for our lives. With the approach of every sunset there is the possibility that a knock at the door may bring grief into our household like an unwelcome guest.

H. Wheeler Robinson finds a hidden meaning in the literal Hebrew of Psalm 30:5 and translates it: "Weeping may come in to lodge at even, but at morn there is a ringing cry of joy." When the cruel guest arrives we can either bolt the door and scream for help (which will be of no avail for there is no way we can keep him out once he knocks) or we can open the door and invite him in. Indeed, if we are Christian we must invite the fearsome guest inside as a part of our witness of our faith in Christ. We do so with the awareness that we are inviting pain and sorrow to be ours. We do not do it because we have learned how to deal with pain and sorrow, but because we know God expects us to face it with faith in him. We do so because we believe that God's grace is sufficient for any trial.

We also know that while the sinister guest brings sadness
there is a coming joy as morning breaks. We know that some
deep purpose can grow out of the brief visit when all is
committed to God. Submissive commitment—this is the key.
As the poet has said:

> One ship drives east and another west,
>   While the selfsame breezes blow;
> 'Tis the set of the sail and not the gale
>   That bids them where to go.
> Like the winds of the air are the ways of fate,
>   As we journey along through life;
> 'Tis the set of the soul that decides the goal
>   And not the storm or the strife.[3]

Let us look into the experience of Jacob and see what God's
hand is able to mold out of the stuff of grief.

Grief has a purifying power—Much of Jacob's life had
been built around continual scheming and deceit. His great
material possessions were proof of the success he had experienced. Most of his life was tainted with self-idolatry. It is the
visitation of grief that once and for all turns him to things
more honorable. The apostle Paul had something of this in
mind: "Finally, brethren, whatsoever things are true, whatsoever things are honest, whatsoever things are just, whatsoever things are pure, whatsoever things are lovely, whatsoever
things are of good report; if there be any virtue, and if there
be any praise, think on these things" (Phil. 4:8).

Grief shows possessions are secondary—When grief drops
in for a visit, the furniture of life becomes terribly unimportant. Whereas they once have been given priority, they suddenly become both useless and comfortless, for they speak
only of this earthly life and have no promise of the life to
come. "The things which are seen are temporal; but the things
which are not seen are eternal" (2 Cor. 4:18).

How often have possessions caused people to neglect the

worship of God and to misuse the sabbath. How many parents have neglected their children's spiritual needs in order to provide more possessions? If grief can turn one to "seek first the kingdom of God," it can be counted as being used by God for good.

Everyone has noticed how hard it is to turn our thoughts to God when everything is going well with us. We "have all we want" is a terrible saying when "all" does not include God. We find God an interruption. As St. Augustine says somewhere, "God wants to give us something, but cannot, because our hands are full—there is nowhere for Him to put it." Or as a friend of mine said, "We regard God as an airman regards his parachute; it is there for emergencies but he hopes he'll never have to use it." Now God, who has made us, knows what we are and that our happiness lies in Him. Yet we will not seek it in Him as long as He leaves us any other resort where it can even plausibly be looked for. While what we call "our own life" remains agreeable we will not surrender it to Him. What then can God do in our interest but make "our own life" less agreeable to us, and take away the plausible sources of false happiness? It is just here, where God's providence seems at first to be most cruel, that the divine humility, the stooping down of the highest, most deserves praise.[4]

Grief shows the value of time—How much is a minute worth? To answer that question, ask yourself what you would give for one more minute with that departed loved one. Few people learn to use time as their most precious possession until grief has brought the solemn realization that man must die. In speaking of pain, which is another form of grief, Buttrick says, "We think then of the expensive toys on which we spend our strength, and we explain, 'What shadows we are, and what shadows we pursue!' Could we ever have known eternity except for the pains of time, or God except for the piercing conviction of our transience?"[5] At best, families are together for all too short a time. We must learn to use it wisely.

Grief highlights the life of faith—The most solid ground

whereon the hurricanes of grief can be faced is that sacred spot to which the will of God has led. If we propose to be Christlike we must realize that pain was very much a part of Christ's ministry. Isaiah said of him, "He is despised and rejected of men; a man of sorrows, and acquainted with grief. . . . Surely he hath borne our griefs, and carried our sorrows: . . . he was wounded for our transgressions, he was bruised for our iniquities: the chastisement of our peace was upon him; and with his stripes we are healed" (53:3–5). Colossians 1:24 gives us Paul's testimony concerning this: "Who now rejoice in my sufferings for you, and fill up that which is behind of the afflictions of Christ in my flesh for his body's sake, which is the church." Christ did not pray for his disciples to be taken out of the world (John 17). This means he envisioned grief, pain, and suffering for his disciples. One cannot live a Christian life apart from all grief because he is called upon to live this life at a time when the "whole world lieth in wickedness" (1 John 5:19).

How often have I heard a bereaved wife say out of a devout heart, "I could not stand this grief if God were not with me." The light of grace is able to penetrate the darkness of grief when stress is placed neither on the lost son, nor the grieving father, but on God who stands in the shadows.

A famous English preacher of the last century tells how he left his home in Liverpool to fill an engagement in Glasgow. The last sight he carried away with him that morning was his little daughter waving her fond and laughing farewell while being held up to the window by her mother. The next day he was stunned by news of his daughter's sudden death, putting out the lamp of his joy. However, as the years went by, the vision of his child waving him farewell returned again and again. It seemed as though God had set her in the window of heaven to beckon him upward to his eternal home. He said, "I would not give that memory for all the gold of earth. I would not part with the inspiration which it stirs within me for all the world could bestow." [6]

It is the life of faith that enables one to see every dark cloud with the light that comes only from the cross. How great are the words of the song:

> Hold Thou Thy cross before my closing eyes;
> Shine thro' the gloom, and point me to the skies:
> Heav'n's morning breaks and earth's vain shadows flee:
> In life, in death, O Lord, abide with me!

If you have found it difficult to feel sorry for Jacob because you know his son Joseph is really still alive, then you can come to understand in a small way how heaven's view of grief may be somewhat different from ours. You and I have read the story and we know Joseph is not dead. We know that soon he shall be reunited with his father. In much the same way we need to remember that God has read our story through and he knows that our departed loved ones are still alive, for they are with him continually (provided, of course, they have found the salvation which is in Christ). When Jacob finally learns that his son still lives he says, "Joseph my son is yet alive: I will go and see him before I die" (Gen. 45:28). Yet, what real difference does it make whether he sees him before death or following death? The greatest promise of the ages is one voiced by Jesus: "I am the resurrection, and the life: he that believeth in me, though he were dead, yet shall he live: and whosoever liveth and believeth in me shall never die" (John 11:25-26). There is no grief which heaven will not heal.

John Greenleaf Whittier's "The Eternal Goodness" says:

> Yet, in the maddening maze of things,
> And tossed by storm and flood,
> To one fixed trust my spirit clings;
> I know that God is good!

. . . .

I long for household voices gone,
    For vanished smiles I long,
But God hath led my dear ones on,
    And He can do no wrong.

I know not what the future hath
    Of marvel or surprise,
Assured alone that life and death
    His mercy underlies.

    . . . .

I know not where His islands lift
    Their fronded palms in air;
I only know I cannot drift
    Beyond His love and care.[9]

Do you seek happiness dependent on chance or on God—
who gives joy to your soul when chance fails? It is often the
failures that open the way to God and wake us from our
slumber. C. S. Lewis remarks, "God whispers to us in our
pleasures, speaks in our conscience, but shouts in our pains: it
is His megaphone to rouse a deaf world. A bad man, happy, is
a man without the least inkling that his actions do not
'answer,' that they are not in accord with the laws of the
universe." [7] Although God's megaphone may be a harsh instrument because there is a possibility it can lead to confirmed
rebellion, it is often man's only opportunity for salvation. At
least "it removes the veil; it plants the flag of truth within the
fortress of the rebel soul." [8] We do well to be sensitive to God
during times of grief lest we miss its message. The tapping of
the Morse code by a telegraph operator is meaningless unless
one learns to decipher the message. It may well be that the
events of grief and sorrow which come into our life are sent in
code by God himself to bring about our ultimate deliverance.

However, it is best not to wait until grief comes to seek out
God. It is best to live with the knowledge that he stands in
the shadows to watch over his own.

5

Why a Thorn?

2 Corinthians 12:7

The thorn of which the apostle Paul writes is physical pain. I say this in spite of the fact that Calvin regarded it as a spiritual temptation; that Luther regarded it as persecution; and that the Roman Catholic view, remaining to this day, regards it as carnal temptation in the matter of taming the sex instinct.

Yet the whole context points to physical pain. The word translated "thorn" most likely refers to a stake such as criminals were often impaled upon. Paul's affliction is like a stake turning and twisting in his body. Just what the physical malady was is not certain. Some say epilepsy of which Julius Caesar, Oliver Cromwell, and Napoleon were also victims. Others feel it was probably recurring attacks of malaria, since the disease was prevalent along the eastern Mediterranean. Perhaps the oldest theory is that of eye trouble causing severe headaches. We do know that after the bright glory experienced on the Damascus road (Acts 9:9) Paul was left temporarily blinded. Paul tells how the Galatian believers would have willingly plucked out their eyes and given them to him (Gal. 4:15). However, the specific disease is not important. Whatever it was, the physical agony was at times unbearable.

Notice there is nothing punitive about the illness. Its torments reside in the body of one who is faithfully serving Christ—"above and beyond" the expected norm. This is a man who has forsaken everything in order to do the will of God.

Notice also that the thorn has not come because Paul has no other hardships. On the contrary, he has quite a load of burdens already. Paul's list of expenditures includes beatings, stoning, shipwreck, perilous journeys, threatened robbery, betrayal by false friends, weariness, anxieties, hunger, thirst, lack of clothes and lodging, and besides all these things, the constant worry and care he carried in his soul on behalf of the welfare of the struggling churches he had established (2 Cor. 11:24–28). Paul reminds us that when it comes to having things to complain about, we will have a hard time competing with him.

The Thorn Confronts Us with Reality

Why the thorn? Let Paul answer this question for himself, and for us: "It helps me keep my feet on the ground [lest I should be exalted above measure]" (2 Cor. 12:7). Paul tells of a spiritual experience he once had (whether actual or visionary he is not sure) in which he was caught up into heaven where he heard and saw things which defy human description (2 Cor. 12:1–4). He is saying that the thorn came lest he consume himself daily in reliving that experience. The thorn brings him back to earth and to reality. Probably none of us will ever have such an experience as Paul's, but every Christian has experienced moments of great inspiration—mountaintop experiences with the Lord—and wanted to echo the words of Peter: "Master, it is good for us to be here: and let us make three tabernacles; one for thee, and one for Moses, and one for Elias" (Mark 9:5).

Most of life must be lived out in the valley. We cannot afford the luxury of a daydream existence. We live among multitudes wrapped in anguish and suffering. If we are to be able to bear witness of Christ to them, we must also know something of their sufferings. Christ does not deliver us from suffering. He does not deliver us from death. The stake (physical pain) reminds us we are mere men. We get sick. We suffer. And some day we shall die. Life is so soon ended.

The Scriptures often connect disease with Satan. Paul does, but he affirms that God is able to use his disease ("the messenger of Satan") for a good purpose—to keep him face to face with reality (2 Cor. 12:7).

The reminder that we are mortal is a call to daily dependence on God. Disease can then become a divine handicap for good. Had it not been for her blindness, Fanny Crosby might never have written "Blessed Assurance, Jesus Is Mine"; or "Jesus, Keep Me Near the Cross," or "To God Be the Glory."

It was from behind prison bars that Paul was able to write some of God's deepest messages, and it was from a heart made sensitive by pain that came the intangible strains that strike the lost chords of our listening souls.

The Thorn Brings Awareness of Grace

Paul was human. No one enjoys pain. He plead with God on three separate occasions (probably during severe attacks) for healing. He found that sometimes healing is not God's will. God's answer was not a miracle, but a promise: "My grace is sufficient for thee: for my strength is made perfect in weakness" (2 Cor. 12:9).

God's grace can be defined in many ways, but here it refers to the gift of his presence. God promises to sustain the suffering believer by his presence. This means in times of greatest weakness one can experience greatest spiritual strength: "Most gladly therefore will I rather glory in my infirmities, that the power of Christ may rest upon me . . . for when I am weak, then am I strong" (vv. 9–10). He who has never been driven to the edge of despair by illness has never seen God's grace in its glorious fulness. It enabled Paul to go contrary to nature and be able to look in favor on his own physical weakness. Strong faith is tempered in the furnace of life's afflictions and hammered out on the anvil of physical agony.

What happens to you in life is not nearly as important as

the response you make. Someone has observed that heat makes a cut flower wilt and a planted one grow. Jesus promised his disciples suffering and trouble—but unspeakable joy. Our selfish ambitions are always coming between us and God's tasks for us. Nothing erases these ambitions like sickness. The lesson the thorn has for us is expressed in one of the great hymns of the church:

> I take, O Cross, thy shadow
>   For my abiding place;
> I ask no other sunshine than
>   The sunshine of His face;
> Content to let the world go by,
>   To know no gain or loss,
> My sinful self my only shame,
>   My glory all the cross.

The world's boot camp trains us to believe that happiness is found only in the spectacular—only in what glitters. The thorn sometimes succeeds in opening our eyes to the unnoticed glory already about us. Luccock tells of a woman watching a beautiful sunset in a small village in India. She exclaimed, "What a wonderful sunset, especially for such a little place." The thorn is God's invitation to do graduate work in the school of prayer. Blind George Matheson once wrote:

My God, I have never thanked thee for my thorn. I have thanked thee one thousand times for my roses, but never once for my thorn. I have been looking forward to a world where I shall get compensation for my cross, but I have never thought of my cross as a present glory. Teach me the glory of my cross. Teach me the value of my thorn. Show me that I have climbed to Thee by the path of pain. Show me that my tears have been my rainbow.[1]

If in God's providence he has chosen to let you show the world how a Christian suffers pain, then clutch your vocation to your breast and thank God for the thorn.

6

The Trial of Faith

Genesis 22

Put your own child to death? Such a thought shocks our
modern minds. Only a mad man would do such a thing or
would suppose that God intended him to do such a thing. We
are even more shocked to find such an episode in the life of
one of the greatest men who ever lived. He is a man known for
his wealth, his honor, but most of all for his faith in God. God
had promised Abraham a son but did not fulfil that promise
until Abraham was one hundred years of age. The promised
son arrived and grew into a healthy young man. Suddenly
God commanded Abraham to sacrifice this son of promise as a
burnt offering.

The fact that we are shocked by such a command merely
points out the difficulty with which we try to place ourselves
in the setting and times of Abraham. It points out what we
often forget—that God had to begin with a very primitive,
fallen race; that he had to begin where they were and then
slowly reveal his way and remake their nature. In this we find
a ray of hope for ourselves, for one thing is certain—God
always begins where we are and then leads us out of the
darkness.

Child-sacrifice was a common ritual in the time of Abraham.
Archaeologists have found much proof of this and such in-
stances are mentioned several times in the Old Testament
(cf. 2 Kings 3:27). Often the firstborn was offered to the gods
so that the hearth might be full, that the woman might bear
many other children, that the land might yield abundant

47

crops, and that the herds and flocks might increase manyfold. Such pagan thoughts came as an effort to placate the unknown gods and elicit their favor. This horrible rite was repeated again and again, generation after generation, until in the midst of such darkness there came the light from a hidden inner voice from God which began to penetrate the consciousness of men.

Therefore, to Abraham, child-sacrifice was seen on every hand and the common standard was that the father had the power of life or death over a child. Thus it was not primarily the conscience of Abraham that clashed with God's command but rather his own heart and affection. No one would have considered Abraham a criminal for performing such an act. This is in some ways a guide for us in our day. God will never direct someone to do what is morally wrong in the thinking of his own time.

What God was saying to Abraham was this: "Do you love me as much as the heathen love their gods?" Now since we know how the story ended we realize that God meant for Abraham to make the sacrifice in spirit only. Actually it is within a person's own attitude that all true sacrifice is first made. There are, therefore, two primary elements involved in God's command. First, God wanted Abraham to have to face up to whether or not his faith was as great as pagan faith. Second, God took this manner of showing that he does not desire human sacrifice but rather the devotion of a living soul. What God wanted Abraham to accept was that Isaac, the son of promise, truly belonged more to God than to Abraham.

Abraham immediately set out for Mount Moriah, which lay three days' journey away. As they arrived at the foot of Moriah, his heart must have ached inwardly, as Isaac remarked that there was wood and fire but no lamb for the sacrifice. Abraham answered, "God will provide." It was not until the last moment that God interposed and did provide—not until

Abraham was "obedient unto death." As Abraham got Isaac arranged for the sacrifice and lifted the knife for the mortal blow, God's voice arrested his hand. Caught in a thicket was a lamb. This was to be the sacrifice.

New Testament writers saw in this event a foreshadowing of the sacrifice of Christ who was God's supreme sacrifice. In 2 Chronicles 3:1, we are told that Moriah is the hill on which Solomon's temple was built. It was the hill containing the threshing floor of Araunah on which David sacrificed to God. It was the hill on which Jerusalem was built, and on one of its lesser summits was a place called Calvary where Christ was crucified. The lamb caught in the thicket was thus a foreshadowing of the Lamb of God (John 1:29) who was sacrificed for the sins of the world.

Although this event is very meaningful to us, Abraham knew nothing of these inner meanings. His was the struggle of a lonely man who realized that his faith was being put to the test. Let us look at this timeless experience of the testing of faith.

The Trial of Faith Comes at Unexpected Moments

"It came to pass after these things, that God did tempt Abraham" (Gen. 22:1). The phrase, "after these things," refers to the previous experiences Abraham has had with God: the promise of Canaan as a homeland; the rescue of Lot from Sodom; the blessing of great material wealth; and at last the birth of Isaac, the son of promise. Abraham has already followed the call of God which has led him away from Ur of the Chaldees and then later away from Haran. Abraham has no doubt felt with each successive venture of faith that nothing further could be asked of him; and yet again and again he finds God still expecting him to increase his faith and to exhibit his faith.

Just as Abraham knew, we too must live knowing that at

every turn in the road our faith may be sorely put to the test.
But at the same time we are assured that in overcoming the
obstacles our faith will grow, for character is possible only
through discipline. What we need to be aware of is that our
faith is tested in the unexpected moments and events of life.
Life ought to take on for us a deeper hue as we realize that
even among the most common occurrences there may come
God's testing of our faith. People in menial tasks may fail to
realize that death and hell are peering in their window. The
day by day events of life are full of meaning and scattered
amidst them are tests for our faith.

The Trial of Faith Makes Unusual Demands

In Genesis 22:2, God says, "Take now thy son, thine only
son Isaac, whom thou lovest, and get thee into the land of
Moriah; and offer him there for a burnt offering upon one of
the mountains which I will tell thee of." Each word seems
carefully chosen to emphasize the tremendous sacrifice that is
asked. Isaac is Abraham's son, his only son, his son whom he
loves supremely. There is always somehow a deeper note of
sadness when a father loses his only son who is to be the heir
of all that the father possesses. The only son has often been
the reason and the motivation behind all that the father has
done. Abraham realizes something of this kind of sadness. All
of his hopes are wrapped up in this one son who has now
reached the threshold of manhood, only to be yielded up. It
has been for Isaac, and God's promise concerning Isaac, that
Abraham has given up his home, his kindred, and a whole
way of life in order to follow the promises of God.

There is no way we can know what went through Abraham's mind. He may have begun to search his soul and pick
out the guilt here and there for which he must have felt that
God was punishing him. He must have questioned whether or
not to obey God, for it would seem difficult for any penalty for

disobedience to be worse than the penalty for obedience. If God wanted to take Isaac, let God do it; for it would be easier to take it that way than for him to voluntarily give up his own child.

Jesus, indeed, spoke difficult words when he said in Matthew 10:37: "He that loveth father or mother more than me is not worthy of me: and he that loveth son or daughter more than me is not worthy of me."

God always asks what you've never done before.—The trial of faith is always the command to do or to be or to give what has never been done before. When Simon Peter, while on the housetop at Joppa, was told to eat what he considered to be unclean meat, his reply was, "Lord, I never have." God is always coming to us and asking us to do what we've never done before.

This comes to us in many ways. Who knows for sure whether honesty is going to be the best policy in a particular case; yet, God demands honesty. God is forever coming to us and asking us to let go of our own leaky life raft, which at least is still keeping us afloat, in order that he may bear us across the murky depths. God gives us everything we have. Then he asks, "Are you willing to give it back to show that I am still the most important thing to you?" A great part of my own spiritual struggle came when God, after having blessed my farming enterprise, asked me to give it up for him.

Abraham had been given a son from whose loins was to come a great nation; now he is asked to give him back. Somehow God is always coming to us and asking that we give up our ace in the hole, which we have just in case God fails, and bet our lives that God will not fail.

God asks without revealing the outcome.—God asked Abraham to offer up his son without telling him that he was merely testing his willingness. In Hebrews 11:17–19, we get a new glimpse of the inner faith of Abraham: "By faith Abraham, when he was tried, offered up Isaac; and he that had received the promises offered up his only begotten son, of whom it was said, That in Isaac shall thy seed be called: accounting that God was able to raise him up, even from the dead; from whence also he received him in a figure." Abraham believed that even if his own son were offered up, God would raise him from the dead, that the promises might still be fulfilled. But God had not so promised. Herein lay the journey of faith. Thus, in effect, Abraham was saying, "Though he slay me, yet will I trust in him" (Job 13:15).

Incidentally, Isaac's faith is no small matter, for he was a young man and could have resisted his aged father. However, he had learned that length of days is not as important as knowing when and how to die. Isaac seemed willing to bid farewell to the earth as he climbed upon God's altar.

The Trial of Faith Spotlights What Is Important

Just as there is a certain amount of friction and rubbing necessary to make a fine polish on a gem, and just as there is a certain amount of bruising and crushing necessary to separate the grain from the straw and chaff, so there is a certain amount of suffering that comes with testing. However, because testing has a way of separating the real from the unimportant it makes us stronger and wiser. When Abraham consented to give his son to God and then joyously was able to receive him back, I am sure from that moment on his love for his son and their relationship together was deeper and more tender. There is nothing that makes us appreciate a loved one more than the prospect of losing him.

True, the ways of God are usually hidden and are not easily discernible at first, but ultimately his will is found to be in line with the purest emotions that are planted in human hearts. When we finally discern the will of God, we find it is not contradictory at all to our best interests. It enables a family to go home together, trusting and obeying in God's graciousness.

As Abraham and Isaac go back down the mountain, it is with a greater awareness than ever before that one can trust himself in the hands of God.

Thus the testing of faith shines a great spotlight upon the importance of God and his promises. For this reason, in the last few verses of Genesis 22, God repeats again his promises to Abraham: "In blessing I will bless thee, and in multiplying I will multiply thy seed as the stars of the heaven, and as the sand which is upon the sea shore; and thy seed shall possess the gate of his enemies; and in thy seed shall all the nations of the earth be blessed; because thou hast obeyed my voice" (vv. 17–18). Now these promises are heard by a much more sensitive Abraham.

What is it that God is asking you to sacrifice? Is it your own hopes for some special career or your own affections toward certain things? You may feel like complaining that no substitute has been provided for your sacrifice—that you have been compelled to lose what was dear as life itself. Even if this be so, when you learn to quietly yield in submissiveness to the hand of God, your loss or pain will take on a new meaning and your whole attitude will be changed. Faith is a way of life which is to be lived even if no substitute is provided. Faith is to be lived even if the ship sinks or the growth is malignant or the heart attack is fatal.

"Whatsoever is born of God overcometh the world: and this is the victory that overcometh the world, even our faith" (1 John 5:4). The world throws many problems and obstacles in our path which only faith in God can overcome. It throws a whole set of standards constantly in our face which would set other things up as being more important than God. Only faith can overcome these. And when at last the world throws up to our failing bodies the challenge of disease and tragedy so that death encompasses us, then it is in that moment of death that

faith grants unto us our greatest victory. For Paul voices our
own convictions, "O death, where is thy sting? O grave, where
is thy victory?" (1 Cor. 15:55).

The Lord does not desire that we suffer pain but that we
learn obedience. God wants us, amidst life, to fit ourselves to
fulfil his will and purposes. We will fail to see the importance
of God in our lives until we, like Abraham, have climbed the
mountain of sacrifice and are able to commit ourselves wholly
to him. The world will offer us many spiritual shortcuts, but
we must always refuse them, because detours are always
rougher than the main road in the long run. God keeps coming
to us and saying that we are to put everything on the line for
him. We make excuses about our weaknesses and past failures,
but God keeps saying that we can begin afresh with him.

> I wish that there were some wonderful place
> In the Land of Beginning Again:
> When all our mistakes and all our heartaches
> And all of our poor selfish grief
> Could be dropped like a shabby old coat at the door
> And never put on again.[1]

This "land of beginning again" is offered at every worship
service where an invitation is given on behalf of God.

God's trial comes in order to present a crisis wherein we can
choose the best. The New Testament tells us that God sent his
own Son to become a final sacrifice for us. Near the same place
where God provided a ram in the place of Isaac, God's only
Son, burdened down with a rough, heavy cross, climbed up a
small steep hill. He was going to his death willingly in order
to bear the sins of the world. In his moment of death he
removed the dread from ours and opened unto us the radiant
glories of eternity. He walked alone up that hill of sacrifice in
order that we might not ever have to walk alone.

God's hand is ever reaching out to touch the lives of those
who are willing to live by faith.

7

Complaints of a Godly Man: Why Do the Wicked Prosper?

Jeremiah 12:1

There comes a time when a person feels that he has stood about all he can stand, and that he has remained silent about as long as he can. There comes a time when it seems that a man can no longer overlook the inequities all about him in life, when he can no longer overlook the ascendancy of evil and the hardship of those seeking to do good. There comes a time when Fitzgerald's description of life seems all too valid: "Life is a football game; everyone is off side, and the rules abolished and the referee chased off the field." [1] There comes a time when a man has to be honest with himself, when these inward cries have to be voiced, and when he has to ask himself, and sometimes even God, the *why* of things.

The words of Jeremiah do not come from a man who is spiritually dull or rebellious, but a man whose conviction of a divine call is such that he affirms that he was called to be a prophet of the Lord even before he was born. This is a man who was denied the joys of a home by God's command not to marry because of the times and his mission. This is a man who stands alone against a rising tide of ungodliness, lustfulness, and the worship of material things—idolatry. He is a lone voice crying out the message of God amid a din of the gleeful chants of those long since ensnared by the devil. He has left family, position, and all things to serve the Lord. Jeremiah's life has been threatened if he continues to preach (Jer. 11:21). His own kin, yes even his own brothers, were a part of the treachery devised against him (12:6).

The Complaints Stated

Why do the wicked prosper?—At least Jeremiah's complaints are straightforward. He begins by saying, "Righteous art thou, O Lord, when I plead with thee: yet let me talk with thee of thy judgments: Wherefore doth the way of the wicked prosper? wherefore are all they happy that deal very treacherously? Thou hast planted them, yea, they have taken root: they grow, yea, they bring forth fruit: thou art near in their mouth, and far from their reins [heart]" (Jer. 12:1–2). Jeremiah begins by saying he knows God is righteous, but on every hand he sees that the wicked prosper, that they are happy, and that they are very secure. This troubles Jeremiah. He says it seems as if God himself planted the wicked in good land and helped them produce abundantly; yet, all the while the Lord seems far from their desires and their hearts, though they do occasionally call his name on their lips. Jeremiah is saying they seem to have everything, and though they may call the name of the Lord, they wouldn't know real religion if it hit them in the face.

Other men have asked such questions. The psalmist said, "I was envious at the foolish, when I saw the prosperity of the wicked. They are not in trouble as other men. They have more than heart could wish. When I thought to know this, it was too painful for me; until I went into the sanctuary of God; then understood I their end" (73:3,5,7,16–17).

Job asked, "Wherefore do the wicked live, become old, yea, are mighty in power?" (21:7). The prosperity of the wicked presents many difficulties to the man who is seeking to live for the Lord. These difficulties are presented to the honest businessman who looks about and sees that measures condemned by the Scriptures appear to bring the best profits. Yet, in the midst of this, he must take the longer look and examine the teaching of history and listen to the words found in Proverbs

15:16: "Better is little with the fear of the Lord than great treasure and trouble therewith." The psalmist is saying, "Don't envy the wicked in his pleasures here in this life, for those are the only pleasures he will ever have."

Why aren't the wicked destroyed?—Jeremiah offers God some free advice: "Pull them out like sheep for the slaughter, and prepare them for the day of slaughter" (12:3). The words "pull out" are used of rending asunder the cords of a tent. Jeremiah thus is asking God to punish the wicked with the speed with which a tent is dismantled and falls to the ground instead of by slow-working processes. In Habakkuk 1:4 we read, "The law is slacked, and judgment doth never go forth: for the wicked doth compass about the righteous; therefore wrong judgment proceedeth." Jeremiah, like the apostle John, wants to ask the Lord to rain down destructive fire and destroy those who speak against him.

Why is faithfulness unrewarded?—Jeremiah reminds the Lord, "Thou, O Lord, knowest me: thou hast seen me, and tried mine heart toward thee." Jeremiah is reminding the Lord of his own genuine sincerity and devotion. Yet, in spite of this knowledge, God is allowing the prophet great hardship. Jeremiah reminds the Lord that the wicked even mock and taunt him as they say, "He shall not see our last end" (12:4). They are saying, "We will outlive you, though you may say 'the wages of sin is death.'"

Jeremiah continues to bemoan the inner falterings of his heart as he speaks of how his inheritance has lost its charm. The brothers of his own family have entered into a conspiracy against him so that he has been forced to forsake his own house. He says that that which should have been his inheritance has become unto him as a lion in the forest which now seeks to destroy him. His inheritance has come to be to him as a speckled bird which, because it is different, has become the object of fierce attack by other birds (12:7–11).

In summary, Jeremiah has fallen into the same pitfall which has since his time engulfed many of us. That pitfall comes by observing God's treatment of others and feeling that we are better judges than God of how they, and we, should be treated. Jeremiah noted that his increased devotions seemed to be met on every hand with increased trials, and he was asking why such should be the case. He was voicing much the same despair as the young prince of Denmark, Hamlet, who cried out in the midst of the circumstances in which he found himself, "O cursed spite that ever I was born to set it right."

What a help it would have been to Jeremiah had he been able to have read 2 Peter 3:3-4, which states: "Knowing this first, that there shall come in the last days scoffers, walking after their own lusts, and saying, Where is the promise of his coming? for since the fathers fell asleep, all things continue as they were from the beginning." This is a warning to us not to be disturbed by scoffers, or the fact that in our own eyes things seem to remain pretty well the same and evil is allowed to go unpunished too long. We must remember we are but creatures of time, while God is the master of it. In his own good time he will make all things right.

The Complaints Answered

God's answer to the complaints of Jeremiah, and, indeed, to our own, are: "If thou hast run with the footmen, and they have wearied thee, then how canst thou contend with horses? and if in the land of peace, wherein thou trustedst, they wearied thee, then how wilt thou do in the swelling of Jordan?" (12:5). The footmen here represent lesser trials and trivial grievances. God is saying, "If you are letting these kinds of things get you down, what will you do when the real difficulties of life come along?"

In much the same sense in which the Lord answered Job out of the whirlwind, God is answering Jeremiah out of the whirlwind. The man who has never experienced a whirlwind of life has not lived very long nor very seriously. God wanted Job to see that though he lived in the midst of the whirlwinds of life, God was in the whirlwinds with him. He is also trying to tell Jeremiah that in the midst of his trials he is not alone.

You are clinging to the world's standard.—This is part of the implication found in God's answer to Jeremiah. Although Jeremiah was a man of great faith, he was tempted, just as you and I are tempted, to judge himself and his success in terms of the world's measure of success. He was, in effect, looking upon his own life and deciding it was a failure because he was not prospering. While this may be the world's standard of success, the Christian must ever remember that true prosperity is progress in the divine life. This means that the Christian cannot say of his business, "This one thing I do." For while he is told to "be not slothful in business," he is told also to "serve the Lord."

Another fault in the thinking of Jeremiah was that he had come to believe that destruction of the evil forces about him was the only way to show their failure. He had fallen into the fallacy of trying to make things add up in this life. The fact that things do not always balance out in this life is found in the parable of the rich man and Lazarus. In this life the rich man had everything and Lazarus had nothing. Had it not been for the words of our Lord we would never have known that in the process of death things were completely reversed.

Belonging to God is more expensive than you once thought.—Jeremiah had begun to feel the pain of belonging to God and not seeing God's kingdom openly triumph. Why do the righteous suffer? To declare the faith of the godly—else the devil taunts, "Doth Job serve God for naught?" But that there may be such men as Job, heroes of the faith—pure, noble, God-fearing souls—God does at times let such men serve him for naught as far as this world is concerned. He hands over this world's wages to the devil, that he may with them bribe, as he in vain tried to bribe our Lord, those who will fall down and worship him.

It was in the midst of trials and whirlwinds of life that the apostle Paul penned Romans 8:28. He went on to explain that the good things work together in order to conform us to the image of Jesus Christ. In 1 Corinthians 4:9, we again hear Paul, amidst whirlwinds in his life, say: "I think that God hath set forth us the apostles last, as it were appointed to death: for we are made a spectacle unto the world, and to angels, and to men." Lieberman gives the following analogy:

The word "spectacle" refers to a stage or theater. Paul is saying that on earth God is putting on a drama. God writes it, directs it, and produces it. The drama plays to a great audience: . . . "the world, and angels, and to men." The Christians are God's actors and actresses. They play the parts that the Director assigns to them and there are in God's eyes no "bit parts" or no leading part, for all are important. Many critics sit in the theater. They watch every move made; they listen to every word spoken and the way it is spoken; they size up the performance and the players. Later, they will write up the review and criticism of the parts the Christians played. Besides that, they will call for the author of the play and applaud Him (if the play is a hit), or criticize Him and the Christians if we muff our lines or underplay our parts.[2]

God's drama, then, shows the world that his children love him even when they suffer. This means that Christian living is more than coming to church and sitting. How many times have I heard someone say, "I sat under the ministry of Brother So-and-So for ten years." This is to lower oneself to the station of a little dog who, when taught to sit, thinks he has done all and deserves a pat on the head. The Lord needs people who are willing to do more for him than sit under the ministry of someone else one hour each Sunday.

This drama of life in which we play demands that we give everything to it. We have not served the Lord and grown in our spiritual life until our service for him means giving up something. Just as there are children who throw tantrums when told they must eat in order to grow, some adults throw tantrums when told they will not grow without giving and making self-sacrifice.

The expensiveness of serving God grows as our understanding of him grows. It is interesting to note that the word in the Bible for tribulation is a word which literally means "friction," or the rubbing necessary to make a fine polish on metal or stone. "Tribulation" was a word used of the crushing of straw and the separating of the grain from the chaff. Tribulation is a painful experience, but out of it comes genuine Christian character.

There are greater trials ahead.—God continues, "If in the land of peace, wherein thou trustedst, they wearied thee, then how wilt thou do in the swelling of Jordan?" (Jer. 12:5). Some interpreters believe the swelling of Jordan refers to the river at flood time. However, it seems more probable that it refers to the dense jungle-type underbrush which swelled out along the banks of the Jordan. Often infested by lions roaming about and fighting with other beasts, this was a dangerous place in which to be. So whatever the meaning, the essential message is the same. God is saying, if when things are going fairly well you have become discouraged and weary, what will you do in the darkness of the night when the real storms come? What will you do when you approach stormy Jordan for the last time? Demosthenes once said, "If they cannot face the candle, what will they do when they see the sun?"

People let minor things rob them of present blessings, even of salvation, by asking, "Why, why, why?" If you are going to be turned aside because the wicked have a larger bank account than you, what will you do when real trouble comes?

Each of us has to learn not to trust in people or things, but in God. It was Emerson who said, "When half-gods go, the gods arrive." When we learn to let the half-gods go, the world's standard of success, and have placed our complete trust in God, we shall also have realized that the wicked will be reckoned with in God's own way. At the root of our complaints about the prosperity of the wicked is the feeling of not being appreciated or rewarded. We must remember that the world has never placed much monetary value on godliness, and never will. Our reward comes from God who does not weigh it out in dollars and cents or gold-plated badges.

A great Christian leader tells a story from his own pastorate. A woman came to him resigning all her positions in the church because, she said, people did not appreciate her efforts. He agreed to accept her resignation, but first asked, "Who were you doing this work for, anyway? If you were doing it for the people's benefit then you are right in resigning, for they have not shown appreciation as they should. If, however, you were doing it for the Lord, then do not worry that your work has gone unnoticed, and do not fret, thinking that you shall have no reward." Our satisfaction is determined by whom we are seeking to please. If God's ultimate purpose were to make you rich, he would do it. But it isn't. His ultimate purpose is to make you Christlike. Therefore, do not envy the prosperous wicked. They have the only heaven they will ever have. Wealth means everything to them. It is rather incidental to the Christian who awaits eternity.

8

The Glory of the Unexpected

Philippians 1:12

Life's design is for our fullest witness. We have a hard time believing this, but it is true. The glory of God's providence shines through in the most unexpected ways. Look at the apostle Paul. As he penned the letter to the church at Philippi, he was in prison at Rome. Now you would think that a preacher's usefulness would abruptly end under such circumstances. Not so! The unexpected glory is that God's providence makes of Paul's imprisonment a wonderful opportunity.

Glory Amidst Confinement

Paul's imprisonment was not in the regular jail. He was permitted to rent his own lodging. His confinement involved being chained night and day to some soldier of the praetorian guard (this was a select group of ten thousand soldiers making up the imperial guard). Can you imagine Paul's delight at having a revolving opportunity to witness to the choicest of Caesar's guards? He would never have been allowed to assemble them for a preaching service, but God's providence allowed him to be chained to them one at a time. Paul explains: "My bonds in Christ are manifest in all the palace [praetorian], and in all other places; and many of the brethren in the Lord, waxing confident by my bonds, are much more bold to speak the word without fear" (Phil. 1:13–14).

No earthly kingdom had the armed might necessary to

penetrate Caesar's household; yet God's providence brings the gospel message by means of the confinement of a Christian. Paul could have chosen to sit in mute silence, dreaming of distant lands needing the gospel. Instead he did what he could, where he was.

The day may come when you, dear reader, will know confinement of one kind or another. It is more likely to be a sickbed than a jail cell. If so, there will be doctors, nurses, and visiting friends to whom you can bear witness of your faith in Christ.

What Paul is saying is that all of life can be one "divine surprise party" after another as we yield to God's providence and find the glory hidden within our earthly limitations.[1] In confident faith Paul speaks of his imprisonment: "I know that this shall turn to my salvation" (Phil. 1:19). Now Paul is not speaking of the salvation of his soul, but rather of his own general well-being as a servant of God. He is certain that at that precise moment he is exactly where God's will has led him. And so he was. Think how poor we would be without Ephesians, Philippians, Colossians, and Philemon, all of which were written during Paul's imprisonment. *Pilgrim's Progress* would never have been written had not John Bunyan been confined in Bedford jail.

The secret to letting the glory shine through any hardship is to be a user of circumstances rather than a prisoner of them. Don't ask, "Why did this happen?" Ask, "What does God expect me to do with these circumstances to further his kingdom?"

Glory Amidst Distress

"I am in a strait betwixt two, having a desire to depart, and to be with Christ; which is far better" (Phil. 1:23). Paul admits he is on the horns of a dilemma, but his dilemma is a rare one: he is not sure which he prefers to do—to live or to die. He finds life like a narrow passageway with walls of rock on each side, allowing no chance to turn aside. He couches the only alternative (death) in words used to speak of taking down a tent or lifting anchor. He is ready to pull up the tent pegs and journey beyond this realm. He is ready to lift anchor and set sail for heaven's shores. Thus he says, "To die is gain" (v. 21).

On the other hand, he finds fulfilment in living in the world as Christ's servant: "For to me to live is Christ" (v. 21). The glory shines through because in either case he will be satisfied. He has faith enough in God's providence to believe that whatever comes of his imprisonment, God can use it to honor his holy name: "Christ shall be magnified in my body, whether it be by life, or by death" (v. 20). Paul's desire is that his life cause the world's gaze to be focused on Christ. He wants his life to be a stage whereon Christ's glory is portrayed. This is the kind of faith that finds glory in unexpected places.

Full of the dreams of youth, Adoniram Judson went to Burma. He labored six years before winning one convert. After twelve years only eighteen souls had yielded to the gospel. One by one he buried his family in the alien soil as hardship and disease engulfed them. He was imprisoned and tortured, often hanging head down so that only his shoulders touched the earth. But upon his death, he left a translation of the Bible in the Burmese language and a host of Burmese Christians. These became his everlasting monument and marked the entrance of the gospel into the pagan darkness of Burma. Through all the distress, the glory shone through.

Glory Amidst Enemies

There are many ways to judge a man's integrity. A great deal can be known about a man by examining a list of his enemies. Now a mature person does not go about making enemies for the fun of it, for there is no virtue, as such, in making enemies. Yet, for the Christian, friendship is impossible with certain philosophies and practices that cut across the message of the Scriptures, and with people who advocate such behavior. The enemies spoken of here are those resulting when a Christian, in a spirit of kindness, takes a stand for the Lord that antagonizes the worldly crowd. Every possibility for the Christian's witness bears with it the possibility of pagan enmity. Paul spoke of this in his correspondence with the church at Corinth: "But I will tarry at Ephesus until Pentecost. For a great door and effectual is opened unto me, and there are many adversaries" (1 Cor. 16:8–9).

The fact that no normal person enjoys bearing the enmity of any person helps explain our usual reluctance to stand for right, against the wrong. Whether the stand is against the gambling racket, liquor traffic, or corruption at city hall, the result is the same. Any time you oppose the devil and his crowd you can expect trouble. The easiest avenue is that of the head-in-the-sand posture made famous by the ostrich. This allows a kind of peace to prevail—but it is the peace of the cemetery. Progress in holiness, righteousness, and spiritual maturity is always disruptive and boat-rocking. Paul did everything possible to live in harmony with the world about him —short of the compromise of his Christian convictions. He tried to be "all things to all men" (1 Cor. 9:22) up to a certain point. Beyond that he stood firm and thus accumulated a long list of enemies. And he had the bruises to prove it.

If enemies are made on the basis of adhering to the demands of the gospel, then they become an evidence of God's approval. Listen to Paul's word about such enemies: "Never in the slightest degree be frightened by your opponents, for such fearlessness will be strong evidence to them of their impending destruction, but to you a sure sign, and that from God, of your salvation" (Phil. 1:28, Williams).

Robert Louis Stevenson wrote that when some people por-

tray St. George fighting the dragon, they make no attempt to
slay him, but tie a pink ribbon about his neck and say, "Nice
pussy," and give him a saucer of milk. Our warfare against
evil must be more deadly. There is such a thing as being rich
in enemies.[2]

Actually we must expect our Christian faith to encounter
difficulties. "For unto you it is given in the behalf of Christ,
not only to believe on him, but also to suffer for his sake"
(Phil. 1:29). Christ's suffering made God's glory available to
us, and our suffering points others to that same glory. Peter
wrote, "Beloved, think it not strange concerning the fiery trial
which is to try you, as though some strange thing happened
unto you: but rejoice, inasmuch as ye are partakers of Christ's
sufferings; that, when his glory shall be revealed, ye may be
glad also with exceeding joy" (1 Peter 4:12-13).

Few stories in the annals of the modern missionary era can
equal that which occurred in one of the remote sections of
Ethiopia.

A few years prior to Mussolini's invasion, several missionaries had penetrated the area of Wallamo and had begun the
task of evangelizing the natives. Slowly they were able to
translate the Gospel of Mark and a few other New Testament
passages into the native dialect. In 1937, in the face of the
advancing Italian army, the missionaries were forced to evac-
uate, leaving behind eighteen baptized converts and the translations of certain portions of the Scriptures which few of the
converts could even read. These immature believers were
harassed and cruelly persecuted, both by the Italians and the
local native rulers. They were beaten unmercifully, forced to
live in hiding, and some were martyred.

Five years later, in 1942, the missionaries were able to
return as the tide of war changed. They feared that no Christian witness would still remain. To their utter amazement,
they found not eighteen Christians, but ten thousand! [3]

An elderly missionary couple were coming home after a lifetime of service on foreign soil. As their ship neared harbor, they wondered whether anyone would be on hand to greet them. When the ship docked, the missionary couple heard the welcoming strains of a band and saw a great throng crowded together on the pier. Thinking they were the objects of the festivities, emotion welled up in their hearts. Suddenly, however, they were pushed aside to make way for a dignitary of the United States and his party who had returned on the same ship from a big game hunt in Africa. By the time the old couple were able to make their way down the gangplank, the cheering crowd and the band were gone. The pier was silent. Discouraged, they made their way to a small hotel. At last the wife broke the silence and said, "We've given our life to the Lord and now after all these years we've come home with not one single soul here to welcome us. I want you to go to our room and ask the Lord why we have been so poorly welcomed."

The old gentleman disappeared up the narrow stairs. Later, when he came down, his wife, still hurt from the rebuff at the dock, said, "Well, what did the Lord say?" Her husband looked at her gently, and with quiet voice answered, "The Lord said, 'Missionary, you're not home yet.' "

God, in his providence, has chosen to give us our final reward beyond earth's portals. Thus death, the greatest enemy of mortal man, becomes the Christian's final doorway to God's glory. This glory which has momentarily broken through during difficult times, shall someday dawn upon us in all its radiant fulness in a most unexpected way (from the world's viewpoint)—by our death! In the meantime, the Bible says, "Being confident of this very thing, that he which hath begun a good work in you will perform it until the day of Jesus Christ" (Phil. 1:6). Oh, the glory of the unexpected!

9

Count Your Many Trials

James 1:2–12

The Bible indicates that a Christian may rephrase a well-known song of thanksgiving as follows: "Count your trials, name them one by one; count your many trials, see what God has done." When you come to the realization that God is able to work good in the midst of trials—that indeed trials can be used to make you more like Christ—then your whole view of trials will change. Trials are one of the things all Christians have in common. What a startling discovery to learn that they can be added up on the credit side instead of on the debit side.

Since trials are sure to come, the important question is: "What will be your attitude toward them?" One thing is certain. Trials will either draw you nearer to God, or they will make you bitter. Thomas Carlyle once said, "The ultimate question posed by life is: Will you be a hero or a coward?" Job's wife advised him to curse God and die. George Bernard Shaw's reaction to the world situation is seen in his statement that if other planets are inhabited they must be using earth for an insane asylum.

Yet into the midst of our groaning and self-pity come the words of James, the half-brother of Jesus, telling us to count outward trials as though they were joyful experiences. He indicates that we will stumble into all kinds of them. The fact that this admonition is foreign to our present outlook merely points out that although the Bible is an ancient book, we have not yet learned its wisdom.

69

Trials and Faith

To begin with, we should look upon trials as things of joy, because trials give us a victorious faith. Trials are "the trying of your faith." [1] Your faith is the target of trials. The words used are those of the smelting of ore in order to remove the dross so that what remains is pure. Life is full of smelters through which a Christian's faith must pass. For the early Christians it was the arena filled with hungry lions. Who knows what ours will be? If the proof of the pudding is in the eating, the proof of our faith is in the testing. Faith is the mark of God's people. Faith brings personal victory. The wayward crowd is always uneasy in the presence of Christian faith. Satan and the world want to see faith die. The Christian is saved by faith, lives by faith; faith is the banner his enemy seeks to strike down. It is faith lived out in daily life for which the natural world has no answer. The bridge is always held in greater regard after the heavy load has passed over it and its strength has been proved.

When faith is tested, there is a wonderful by-product that comes, and that by-product is patience (James 1:3). We usually think of patience as that quality of being able to sit all day fishing without even having a nibble. Nothing could be further from what James had in mind. Biblical patience has in it the idea of endurance or steadfastness. It is a word used of a soldier who, though burdened down with his heavy pack, continues to plod ahead without giving up. He goes again and again into battle without deserting. There are millions of Christians who have given up, deserted, thrown down their packs. Ask them why and you will receive many excuses—dislike for some teacher or preacher; they felt ignored; the church budget wasn't right, they didn't get their own way; or, they experienced sickness or tragedy—but whatever the excuse, any surrender is a paltry one. Patience is staying power when life tumbles in on you.

I saw patience in action as I stayed at a hospital throughout a long night vigil. A wife watched her husband's life slowly ebb away. The man was a local police desk sergeant. A wild young man, brandishing a shotgun, had stormed in and shot him at close range. Later it was learned that the young villain was trying to help his brother break out of jail. But his brother was in a different jail altogether. Just as the first hint of daybreak appeared, the sergeant, after a night of laborious breathing and an agonizing struggle for life, needlessly passed beyond this earthly realm. To add to her sorrow, this was the second husband this fine Christian woman had lost tragically. Her calm, determined faith in the face of such deep loss was an inspiration. Previous trials had wrought out in her a patience —a staying power. She had nothing but thankfulness to God in her heart that God had given them the brief happiness that had been theirs, and that her husband was a man of faith who had claimed the wonderful promises of eternity.

James assures us that such patience works out in us a complete Christian maturity: "Let patience have her complete work, that ye may be whole and fully mature, falling short in no area of life" (1:4, my translation). To allow faith's trials to produce such endurance, and to allow such a spirit of endurance to mold us into fully mature Christians, is a painful process. It is like lying on an operating table and letting the surgeon's knife cut deep without shrinking or screaming. The child becomes a man only after many bumps and bruises, after many chastenings and trials. The alternative to faithful Christian endurance is not only to follow the advice of Job's wife to "curse God and die"; it is also to be guilty of Satan's accusation that Job served God only for what he got out of it.

Trials and Your Outlook

Of course the big question is, "How do you joyfully face trials in such a way that faith is strengthened and endurance manifested?" There are some resources available. To begin with, a certain attitude is basic. It is not natural to look upon trials as blessings. The apostle James, inspired by the Holy Spirit, recognizes the difficulty and says, "If any of you lack wisdom, let him ask of God, that giveth to all men liberally, and upbraideth not; and it shall be given him" (1:5). The wisdom referred to is the ability to recognize trials as blessings.

The Christian method of keeping books involves knowing how to count our troubles—knowing where they belong on the ledger. This peculiar bookkeeping requires a wisdom which is God-given. Such wisdom involves an understanding of the importance of the moral and the eternal. It means an evaluation of life that realizes pleasure is not a sound standard for weighing life, that abiding happiness is wrought by being molded into the likeness of Christ. In this light, many of the so-called "gay times" should be put on the debit side of the ledger, for they separate us from God and his will for our lives. Sometimes a better job or a new promotion belongs on the debit side because it makes us too busy to serve God.

Since such wisdom is God-given, it can only come through prayer. As James indicates, if you want this kind of wisdom, ask God for it. Let me pause to remind you of the danger involved here. Don't ask God for such an outlook unless you really want it, for God gives "liberally and upbraideth not." Your banker may feel that you have not handled your finances properly and thus may upbraid you when you come seeking a loan. A husband may upbraid his wife when she asks for shopping money. But when you ask God for wisdom to see the real values of life, and of trials, he will give it liberally. The moral wisdom in question is the great deficiency in the average Christian's life. It is the sum of practical living. It is being able to discern between the earthly and the heavenly. Once obtained, this wisdom casts such an illumination on life that you will never again desire the paths of unrighteousness nor the luxury of irresponsibility. It will ruin you as a worldling. It will leave you with a lot of slightly used equipment on hand. There is no purpose in asking God to make you a good doctor or lawyer unless you are willing to go to school. Neither is there any purpose in asking God for an outlook and wisdom that demands a change of values unless you are willing for your values to be changed. This is what James has in mind when he warns: "Let him ask in faith, nothing wavering. For he that wavereth is like a wave of the sea driven with the wind and tossed. For let not that man think that he shall receive any thing of the Lord. A double-minded man is unstable in all his ways" (1:6–8).

James is warning against praying for an outlook which you don't really want. This makes a farce out of prayer. It is like praying that God will make you Christlike when down deep you prefer to be worldly. The word translated "wavering" literally means to be torn between two judgments or sets of values. To pray in faith is to pray in total commitment. There is no place in prayer for indecision as to the value of the object desired. Such indecision is like an uncertain wave on the sea which is blown first one way and then the other by the changing winds. The phrase translated "a double-minded man" literally means a man with two souls who has not yet decided what kind of man he wants to be. Such a man may just as well save his breath, for his prayer is a farce.

Trials and False Values

Not only do trials make possible a victorious faith but they erase man-made distinctions and values. The apostle James uses the matter of poverty and wealth as an illustration: "Let the brother of low degree rejoice in that he is exalted: but the rich, in that he is made low: because as the flower of the grass he shall pass away. For the sun is no sooner risen with a burning heat, but it withereth the grass, and the flower thereof falleth, and the grace of the fashion of it perisheth: so also shall the rich man fade away in his ways" (1:9–11).

The poor man should see that through Christ he is exalted as a child of God. The rich man should see that in Christ he is no richer than anyone else. Both need to see that their worth depends upon serving God, that faith erases the despondency of the poor and the pride of the rich. They need to see that all of life quickly wilts like the summer grass before the scorching winds. The trial of faith has a way of sweeping away the temporary tinsel that adorns so much of life.

One of my seminary professors skimped and saved in order to build a new home for his family. Only weeks after moving into the new home, one of his children became critically ill. There was the possibility of the loss of a limb. This professor remarked that he would gladly give the key to his new home to someone else if it could mean his child could walk again. Trials point out for us the things that really count and we are the richer because of this. Trials are a reminder that you can't take it with you.

Trials and the Crown

Contrary to popular opinion, trials place a crown on life that nothing else can. Hear James as he continues, "Blessed is the man that endureth temptation: for when he is tried, he shall receive the crown of life, which the Lord hath promised to them that love him" (1:12).

During a revival in a small rural church I was made aware of how the promises of the Bible are misread and misunderstood. An elderly, almost illiterate man was bringing a devotional to his class. He read this verse as follows: "Blessed is the man that endureth temptation: for when he is *tired* he shall receive the crown of life." His bent body and calloused hands indicated that he knew what it was to be tired. I have often wondered what that verse really meant to him. Literally, the promise is to the one who has passed through the fire of testing and has remained faithful. He has stood the test as genuine gold ore withstands the smelting fires.

The promise involves a "crown of life." In Greek grammar this is a genitive of apposition, so the meaning is "a crown which is life." "Life" and "crown" are here identical. There are different levels and degrees of life. For some people, life never rises above the animal level. However, to the child of God life takes on a different light. Every trial adds depth and meaning. Every trial contributes to the purification of life. In addition to endless life, eternal life has at its foundation the idea of a different quality of life. Perhaps Revelation 4:10 helps explain the figure of speech. In the vision of heaven, the writer sees twenty-four elders who in a song of praise cast their crowns before the throne of God.

The symbol of victory for a Christian is neither a laurel crown nor a bejeweled one. Rather it is a life purified and perfected by trials—a life which is its own crown and which some day can be cast in praise before the throne of God. Such a life is the only trophy which can be presented to God.

This means that "count your many blessings" and "count your many trials" are nearer the same than one would at first suspect. The Bible tells us to use a system of bookkeeping that will enable us to put trials down on the credit side—to be thankful for them. They refine us and turn us to God. Sidney Lanier, broken by the ravages of disease, found a faith that enabled him to write:

> As the marsh-hen secretly builds on the watery sod,
> Behold I will build me a nest on the greatness of God.

Trials are coming. Your attitude toward them will determine whether they will break you or make you.

10

Getting What You Need

Philippians 4:19

Socrates often walked in the busy marketplace of Athens asking both buyers and sellers, "Can you tell me where those things can be bought that are *really* necessary to life?" A group of well-known American financiers met in Chicago in the early 1920's. They had under their control more money than was deposited in the national treasury. Twenty-five years later, in his syndicated newspaper column, Billy Rose called the roll of this group of financial giants. The man who had cornered millions through wheat speculation had died abroad, insolvent. The president of the nation's largest independent steel company had died penniless. The president of the New York Stock Exchange had just been released from prison. A cabinet member during Harding's administration had just died, after having been released, for health reasons, from prison. The greatest exploiter of the "bear" market in Wall Street had committed suicide. The leader of the world's greatest monopoly, the production of matches, had likewise committed suicide. Billy Rose concluded: "All of these men had learned how to make big money, but not one of them had learned how to live." [1]

At the beginning of the twentieth century the average American wanted 72 different things and considered 18 of them necessary. By 1950, Mr. Average American had 496 wants and felt 96 of them were necessary.[2]

All of this indicates that man has never found it easy to learn what is necessary for happiness—what he really needs and must have. Most of us are so busy scheming and fighting and clawing for a place in the earth where we can live fully and happily that we fail to hear the astonishing statement from the lips of the apostle Paul: "My God will supply all that you need from his glorious resources in Christ Jesus" (Phillips). God is not hereby promising to provide us with everything we want, but rather with what we need. There is a difference. The promise is that as every need arises, one day at a time, God is able to supply (fill up) that need. What are the needs of every person who desires a full life? An investigation of Philippians 4 reveals the answers.

Peace

Your basic need is the "peace of God, which passeth all understanding [far excels . . . imagination]" (Phil. 4:7). We must keep in mind that the real needs of a full life can be supplied *only* by God. Peace is a perfect example. This is the peace which comes from God when, through Christ, we make peace with God. Peace comes through unconditional surrender to Christ. This peace has a very important daily function. It "shall keep your hearts and minds through Christ Jesus" (v. 7). The word translated "keep" literally means to stand as a sentinel, to serve as a lookout. As the apostle penned these lines he was himself a prisoner of Caesar. No one could take him away because the emperor kept him guarded constantly. In the same fashion, God's peace is able to guard your heart and mind from those things which would destroy happiness— those competitive interests that strive to have God's place on the throne of your heart. Jeremiah warned, "The heart is deceitful above all things, and desperately wicked: who can know it?" (17:9). Our hearts need to be garrisoned by God's peace. Only God's peace makes possible the admonition: "Rejoice in the Lord alway: and again I say, Rejoice. Let your moderation be known unto all men. The Lord is at hand. Be careful for nothing; but in every thing by prayer and supplication with thanksgiving let your requests be made known unto God" (Phil. 4:4-6).

The idea is that life should be a season of rejoicing in which the Christian is to reveal openly his strong convictions, though in a gracious manner. "Moderation" has this literal meaning rather than that usually given it of being flimsy and undecided. Many advocate moderation and by it mean one is not to totally abstain from anything. Early Christians were known for their unwavering convictions. The younger Pliny, describing the Christians to the Roman emperor, said they were obstinate as pigs.[3] A valid reason for joyful faithfulness is, "The Lord is at hand" (Phil. 4:5).

The nearness of God as he guards our hearts and minds also makes possible the admonition, "Be careful for nothing." The Bible is literally saying, "Stop being filled with anxiety about everything." Perhaps the biggest enemy of happiness is anxiety. It is a blight that can wither all of life.

Reinhold Niebuhr[4] says that anxiety is the result of man's being both free and limited—free to choose, yet finite and capable of wrong choice.

Paul Tillich[5] understands anxiety to be "the state in which a being is aware of its possible nonbeing." In other words, the realization of the possibility of death causes a natural anxiety. Tillich observes that the form taken by anxiety varies in different periods of history according to whatever is seen to pose the greatest threat to existence. He lists three critical periods. As the Greek civilization was crumbling, the absolute threat was death brought on by fate. During the Reformation era, the absolute threat was condemnation brought about by guilt. In our contemporary world, the absolute threat is meaninglessness brought about by emptiness. Tillich is not saying that these are absolute categories, for they all exist to some degree in every age. The difference is one of predominance. Tillich speaks of the possibility of anxiety running amuck so that it becomes neurotic by becoming concerned about certain circumstances or problems other than the possibility of death. He seems to indicate that if one faces up to his anxiety about death, he need not become a victim of neurotic anxieties. At any rate, this is the biblical solution to anxiety.

The Bible indicates there are certain things which do not deserve our anxiety. The Greek word (*merimnon* is the verb; *merimna* the noun) used in the New Testament passages on anxiety is usually translated "take thought for." It means to be filled with cares and anxieties. Jesus said that Martha was too anxious about little details (Luke 10:41). He warned his disciples not to worry about how to answer charges brought against them (Luke 12:11). In the Sermon on the Mount Jesus said his followers should not be consumed with anxieties about the physical needs of life—food and clothes (Matt. 6:25). He went on to say that a Christian should not be overly worried about the future: "Take therefore no thought [be not anxious] for the morrow: for the morrow shall take thought [be anxious] for the things of itself. Sufficient unto the day is the evil thereof" (v. 34). Jesus is not saying that Christians should not work hard and make plans. But he is saying that Christians have settled the matter of death and judgment and, therefore, must learn to live in faith, one day at a time, that God who is sufficient today will also be sufficient tomorrow.

Most people agree that first things should be put first. Disagreement comes at what constitutes "first things." I remember speaking with a woman who, along with her husband and two sons, was without Christ. Her excuse was that in order to make the kind of living they needed they had to work seven days a week. She concluded by saying, "You just have to put first things first." Her first things were different from those of Christ who said, "Seek ye first the kingdom of God, and his righteousness; and all these things shall be added unto you" (v. 33).

On the other hand, there are some things which constitute valid anxieties. The Bible indicates that fellow church members should care about one another's welfare (1 Cor. 12:25). Paul himself speaks of his constant anxiety for the churches he had established (2 Cor. 11:28). The Bible draws a line between the material and the spiritual. One is to be anxious about the spiritual, beginning with one's own soul. When this anxiety is answered through faith in Christ, one is to be anxious about the church, as it seeks to share the gospel message, and about those who yet live in spiritual darkness. But one is not to be consumed with anxieties about material possessions and the uncertainty of tomorrow.

The fact that the great masses are ignorant of the biblical answer to anxieties is evidenced by the statement of Halford Luccock: "Telling our generation to have no anxiety about anything seems offhand like telling a company of people sitting on the edge of the crater of an active volcano to be not anxious. To the many anxieties of private life we have added the anxieties over human survival, or an obliterating nuclear war. In these days of potential strife with hydrogen bombs and long-range missiles, we feel strongly that there is 'no place to hide,' not even in the most remote spot of earth." [6]

There never has been a place to hide from life, and if there were that would not be the answer. The following is an illustrative bit of irony:

There was in Australia during the 1930's a scholar of world events who foresaw that a great war was sure to break out. He realized that Japan would be one of the belligerents. . . . Accordingly this twentieth-century wise man studied the atlas in search of the perfect hiding place, the best possible island of escape from the storm about to break across the civilized world. By the employment of careful logic and the process of deduction, he finally selected the spot, an obscure virtually uninhabited island, and in the summer of 1939 he went ashore there. The name of the island was Guadalcanal!" [7]

Escape is no answer. It is more important to face anxieties and to realize that one does not stand alone. Casting "all your care [anxieties] upon him; for he careth for you" (1 Peter 5:7). Instead of worrying we should, with a thankful spirit, pray to God about our problems, questions, and needs. We should share these things with God instead of storing them up in anxiety. "In every thing by prayer and supplication with thanksgiving let your requests [questions] be made known unto God" (Phil. 4:6). This is the kind of attitude necessary to let God's peace guard our hearts and minds.

Companionship

Another necessity of life is companionship. No one likes to go it alone. Our computer age is constantly seeking to reduce each of us to a number or a perforated card. Paul speaks to the need of companionship: "Those things, which ye have both learned, and received, and heard, and seen in me, do: and the *God of peace shall be with you*" (Phil. 4:9).

The indication is that we must do something in order to experience the companionship of God. We are to act. Paul continues: "Finally, brethren, whatsoever things are true, whatsoever things are honest, whatsoever things are just, whatsoever things are pure, whatsoever things are lovely [worthy of admiration], whatsoever things are of good report; if there be any virtue [N.T. word for ethics], and if there be any praise, *think on these things*" (v. 8). Someone has observed, "Ten percent of the people think. Twenty percent think they think. And the rest would rather die than think." [8] The word translated "think" means here to fix your mind on, to latch onto. In its background is the idea of adding up the values and committing oneself to them. It is very easy for an "open mind" to be filled with the trivial and the smutty. There are some thoughts that should be kicked in the teeth as soon as they appear on the premises. If you desire the companionship of God, you must be committed to the good and the pure. You must be able to distinguish the profane from the eternal. Some people rush through life like foolish travelers who sleep in the day and drive at night, bypassing the wondrous sights.

Of course God has promised to be with a Christian every moment. But there is not only the matter of our being *aware* of his presence, there is also a difference in the way God is present. If we are perennially indifferent or wayward, then God is present to condemn and convict our conscience. However, if we are willing to honestly examine ourselves, God is able to be present in a comforting companionship.

It is said that when Queen Elizabeth grew old and time had ravaged her beauty, the mint master made the mistake of making her likeness on the coins too accurate. He was disgraced and the shilling die was broken. Only one mutilated specimen is in existence. Her maids took the hint and removed all mirrors from the palace. A magazine of the times reported that the queen "had not the heart to look herself in the face for the last twenty years of her life." [9] The Bible warns against refusing to see ourselves as we really are: "If any be a hearer of the word, and not a doer, he is like unto a man beholding his natural face in a glass: for he beholdeth himself, and goeth his way, and straightway forgetteth what manner of man he was" (James 1:23–24).

We need God's companionship, but the price is dedication and honest self-examination.

Contentment

The difference between happiness and unhappiness is neither wealth nor position; it is contentment. "I have learned, in whatsoever state I am, therewith to be content" (Phil. 4:11). Paul goes on to say that whether his river goes dry or runs bank full, whether he is starving or feasting, he is content. He uses words found in the background of the Greek mystery religions to indicate that he has been initiated. Both trials and prosperity have taught him the secret of contentment.

The word translated "content" (*autarkeia*) is from the Stoic vocabulary. The Stoics meant by it a state of mind in which a man is completely independent of all things and people—self-sufficiency to the ultimate degree. The Stoic proposed to become self-sufficient by eliminating all desire so that no person or thing was held dear. Epictetus said, "Begin with a cup or a household utensil; if it breaks, say, 'I don't care.' Go on to a horse or pet dog; if anything happens to it, say, 'I don't care.' Go on to yourself, and if you are hurt or injured in any way, say, 'I don't care.' If you go on long enough, and if you try hard enough, you will come to a stage when you can watch your nearest and dearest suffer and die, and say, 'I don't care.'" No wonder T. R. Glover said, "The Stoics made of the heart a desert, and called it peace." [10]

Paul's contentment differs radically from that of the Stoics. The Stoic gained contentment through self-sufficiency; Paul gained contentment through God-sufficiency. It is not a human achievement. It is a gift of God. It does not depend on outward circumstances for the full life. It rather depends on God's sufficiency, whatever the circumstances.

Power

It is the same God-sufficiency which makes possible our saying, with Paul, "I can do all things through Christ which strengtheneth me" (Phil. 4:13). This is real power for living, power for any task, because it is Christ's power. The word translated "strengtheneth" has the same root from which comes our word "dynamo." This does not mean we can do

anything our whimsical desires may dictate. The promise is
that we can do anything God expects of us. We are given the
power to do his will. We are given the power for honest living,
faithful service, victory over evil habits and temptations. This
erases the excuse, "I know I ought to, but I just can't."

Peace, companionship, contentment, and power are our
basic needs. Only God can supply them. If you wait for the
world to fill the vacuum left by the absence of these needs,
your life will remain empty.

Paul prefaces the passage we have discussed by reminding
the Philippians (4:3) that their names are written in the "book
of life." God delivers us from being listed only in earthly
books, whether a tax collector's book, bankbook, social regis-
ter, or who's who. But the same God who writes our names on
heaven's roll is able to meet our every need in this life. And he
does it with a grandeur that befits his glory—in accord with
his riches. A bum who offers his help does not give us much
encouragement, for we know his limitations. "But my God
shall supply all your need *according to his riches* in glory by
Christ Jesus."

Keep in mind that as Paul speaks of God's power to supply
our needs, he is an obscure prisoner of Caesar. "But this
obscure prisoner who has planted the gospel in Caesar's
household has won more eternal fame and power than all the
Caesars combined. Nero will commit suicide shortly after Paul
has been executed. Nero's star went down and Paul's rose and
rises still." [11]

11

Grasping for Glory
(On Human Terms)

Genesis 11:4

The account of the confusion of tongues or the origin of diversified languages is found in Genesis 11. History and archaeology bear clear testimony to the fact of the confusion of languages and many scholars feel that all languages can be traced back linguistically to one common language. Yet if we bypass this account so quickly, we miss its message.

It seems probable (v. 4) that God had told Noah's sons to scatter across the face of the earth and to subdue it. Instead, mankind congregates and plans to build a tower and a city. Now a city in that day was as a nation today. The location of this project is said to be Shinar which is the Hebrew name for lower Mesopotamia, the area of Babylon. The tower was undoubtedly a ziggurat, a pagan temple, built with seven levels and crowned with a pagan temple for worship. There are remains of similar types of ziggurats today, although the one mentioned here has long since disappeared. However, the excavator of Babylon, Robert Koldewey, has gathered certain architectural evidence which, together with information found in the cuneiform sources and in the writings of Herodotus, indicates that the name of one tower in Babylon was E-te-men-an-ki, meaning "house of the foundation of heaven and earth." Standing in a large enclosure of some fifteen hundred feet square, it was erected upon a square foundation, each side being three hundred feet long. The interior was of dried brick while the outer layer of the walls, nearly fifty feet thick, was of baked brick. According to the cuneiform record, as well as

85

the writings of Herodotus, the tower rose in seven stories, each story being slightly smaller in area than the previous one, to a height of almost three hundred feet, making it second only to the great pyramids of Egypt. During the reigns of Nabopolassar and Nebuchadnezzar this structure apparently attained its greatest magnificence, and the temple on top was covered with blue enameled tile. Thus we see man, scheming to build himself a walled city, with his own pagan temple in it, that he may make for himself a name by which to be remembered.

A Contagious Disease of Giantism

When men have the disease of giantism they must constantly build towers to convince themselves of their own superiority. Down deep they can never really believe in their own greatness. A man thus afflicted "looks at the pinnacle of his gigantic tower, and as, several millenniums later, he points somewhat familiarly and jovially to the stars where he will soon establish his vegetable garden, he says to himself: 'All this thou hast accomplished, O holy, glowing heart.' " [1]

Certain symptoms make a diagnosis of giantism fairly easy. The first is that of an ungodly ambition. This means an ambition which does not take God into account. Genesis 11:4 calls to mind one of the indictments of Genesis 6, wherein sinful humanity is composed of "men of renown" which may well be translated "men of the name." Ambition is a terrible master who never sleeps. Unless ambition is determined by some standard of righteousness it will destroy the soul. Take the spiritual element out of ambition and only ruthlessness remains.

The temptation to try to create an earthly heaven is an ever-present one. Instead of clay bricks, the Greeks built an earthly heaven out of knowledge (which is merely the use of a different building material). Yet the Bible warns: "Hath not God made foolish the wisdom of this world? For after that in the wisdom of God the world by wisdom knew not God, it pleased God by the foolishness of preaching to save them that believe" (1 Cor. 1:20–21).

Rome sought to build an empire out of military conquest. At the top of the empire stood the Caesar who set himself forth as divine. Man is ever getting a glimpse of God's throne and trying to climb up and sit on it. I recently read an article by a space-conscious man who maintains that the "old faith" is passing away and that we will develop a pantheism which will be more favorable to the scientific age. This idea that nature can be deified is a prevalent one and is merely the veiled pride of men who claim to have the answer to every need. Following the launching of the first sputnik, the East Berlin *Frei Welt* proclaimed this boast: "The eighth day of creation has begun. The Bible tells about the seven others, and what is said is but a dream of fantasy. But the eighth day of creation, which has given to the earth its second moon, is a reality, a true act of socialistic creativity. With such the Bible cannot compete." [2]

Hitler proclaimed that the Third Reich would last for a thousand years. With blind pride we ever proclaim "America, God's country." Amidst all our goals we would do well to remember one set forth by the apostle Paul: "I press toward the mark for the prize of the high calling of God in Christ Jesus" (Phil. 3:14). This is truly a worthy ambition.

Another symptom of giantism is rebellion. It comes quietly and gradually so that one is not aware of its stealthy approach. As mentioned previously, Genesis 11:4 implies an awareness that God's will involved the scattering of men across the face of the earth. In contrast, the desire of men involves a plan which would prevent such scattering—"lest we be scattered abroad upon the face of the whole earth." The rebellion of the prodigal son did not come all with one blow but gradually piled up until it became a heavy burden.

Rebellion begins with the question, "Why shouldn't I be able to do it?" Its culmination comes with the statement, "I'll do as I please and it's nobody's business—not even God's." The rebellion of the tower builders, like that of the prodigal son, is the world's same old story, endlessly repeated with only the addition of new personalities. There is always the same ending. We are forever sacking up God's gifts as though they were the attainment of our own cleverness and crating them off to misuse them. Somehow we still prefer our own crumbling staircase instead of God's straight and narrow path.

A Sinister Agreement

In Genesis 11:4, Moffatt correctly captures the spirit of the verse as he begins his translation, "Come on." "Oh, come on," the cry of rabble-rousers, has led many down the lighted path to eternal darkness. "Oh, come on, let's stay together and make a name for ourselves right here without worrying about what God wants." This seems to be the tenor of the passage. Some have conjectured that the earth's population may have numbered about thirty thousand. At any rate, there was still only one language; and with this one language there seemed to be a unanimous movement—in the wrong direction.

The sinister agreement involves taking command of God's earth. The divine command "to subdue the earth" can be carried to extremes. God intended by this command that men should make use of the earth in such a way as to glorify his holy name. Carried to an extreme, men suddenly subdued the earth to make themselves a name and to glorify themselves. When such is the case, God merely becomes a source of embarrassment which is best kept hidden.

The sinister agreement involves becoming a candidate for the office of God. While not actually having cards printed with the statement, "I am running for God," this is basically what is involved when man flies in the face of God's will. The tower represents an effort to build one's own little world. When we cease to be dependent upon God we fall into the same pitfall Nietzsche fell into. In his book *Joyful Wisdom*, he has "the Madman" go out with a lighted lantern in broad daylight to search for God. The Madman finally declares that God is dead. He goes on to say, "We have killed him." The Madman concludes by saying, "Is not the magnitude of this deed too great for us? Shall we not ourselves have to become gods, merely to become worthy of it?" Thus when we do away with God in our lives we of necessity become a candidate for the office.

Man is never more unpredictable than when he cuts himself loose from God. He has no standard by which to act. His word is utterly worthless. He is doomed to misdirection because of an ever oscillating compass.

God's Inspection

Genesis 11:5 is filled with satire: "The Lord came down to see the city and the tower, which the children of men builded." It is not that God was not able to discern what men were up to, but rather it points out the lilliputian nature of man's attempts to build his own world. What man thinks is a colossal structure is so small that from the glory of heaven it looks like the work of ants. The psalmist pictures something of this as he says, "The kings of the earth set themselves, and the rulers take counsel together, against the Lord. . . . He that sitteth in the heavens shall laugh: the Lord shall have them in derision" (2:2–4).

Be sure of this: God will examine every deed. Just as a new suit often bears a tag stating who examined it for flaws, so everything must have upon it the stamp of God's approval or disapproval. God examines our ledgers, our homes, our notes, our desires, and our purposes. Closed doors and locked vaults are no hindrance to God's inspection. Something of this is seen in the statement, "We must all appear before the judgment seat of Christ" (2 Cor. 5:10).

We also need to remember that the God who inspects everything is the same God who writes the rules of history. History is the story of God's planting and God's plucking up. When, as at Babel, men have banished God from their thoughts, they find there is nothing really lasting that can hold them together. A nation's unity and strength is based upon God in her midst. Nations which forget this cease to exist. When the cities of men become more desirous of "things" than the city of God we are doomed. God then comes to dig up every root and pour salt on the ground which produced the harvest of indifference.

We make the mistake of thinking that if God doesn't immediately rap our knuckles we have succeeded in deceiving him. Judgment often comes slowly. In fact this was true at Babel. It probably took years to make the brick, burn them, lay them, and build a city and a tower. Since time is in the hand of God, he can afford to wait. God has allowed many a man to make brick and build for a lifetime his own little tower only to come in the last moment and have it tumble. When a man's total life has been invested in what he has built with his own hands, all that is left melts with the perennial rains and decays back into the dust.

God recognizes our desire for remembrance and permanence, and in fact has made such a thing possible. The book of life spoken of in the Bible is God's promise of an eternal remembrance for those who have lived by faith. The heavenly city spoken of in the Bible is prepared for those who have followed the King of kings and Lord of lords while on this earth. All of eternity is promised to those who are willing to "lose their life." The sin of Eden and the sin of Babel are basically the same sins. They picture the attempts of men to escape from dependence on God. They picture men reaching out for "remembrance" by cutting themselves off from the only possibility of real remembrance.

> We are all blind, until we see
> That in the human plan
> Nothing is worth the making if
> It does not make the man.
>
> Why build these cities glorious
> If man unbuilded goes?
> In vain we build the work, unless
> The builder also grows.[3]

Whale observes that the counterpart to Babel is found in the meaning of the day of Pentecost. "When men's hearts are failing them for fear of that which may be coming upon the earth, they build their towers of Babel and cry, as Swinburne did, 'Glory to man in the highest, for man is the master of things.'"[4] Whereas Babel is the symbol of human confusion, Pentecost is the symbol of unity and purpose which comes through God. On the day of Pentecost God's Holy Spirit came to empower the early Christians for the sharing of the good news of salvation in Jesus Christ. The good news had been announced at the birth of Christ by the angels, who proclaimed, "Glory to God in the highest."

The answer to the estrangement between God and man is found in the message of the gospel as it is interpreted to the human heart by God's Holy Spirit. There is nothing wrong with building earthly towers as long as they are built within the will of God and for his glory. As Ralph L. Murray reminds us, "Earth can be the gate of heaven or the avenue of hell."[5] In the literal Hebrew of Genesis 11:9 there is a play on words which is captured by J. M. Powis Smith in the *Complete Bible, An American Translation:* "That was why its name was called Babel, because it was there that the Lord made a babble of the language of the whole earth." Man is never more confused than when he proposes to stand as a god. The towers which men build are so often only empty monuments to the illusion which has been theirs. Jesus talked of a rich farmer who confused his farms with his soul and became so identified with his farms that he lost his soul. Such a person falls into the same outlook found in the inscription which Thomas Smith, a stonecutter, placed on his wife's monument in North Carolina about eighty years ago: "Here lies Jane Smith, wife of Thomas Smith, marble cutter. This monument was erected by her husband as a tribute to her memory and a specimen of his work. Monuments of the same style, $350." [6]

The Egyptian pharaohs built great statues and obelisks chiseled with the record of their honors lest men forget them. They built pyramids as tombs lest they be forgotten, but the tombs stand rifled and empty among the barren sands of a civilization long since decayed.

Men who seek to be remembered by making a name for themselves need to remember that "there is none other name under heaven given among men, whereby we must be saved" (Acts 4:12); and, it is only through a faith commitment to Jesus Christ that there can be an eternal remembrance and eternal life. Concerning this Jesus, the Bible says: "God also hath highly exalted him, and given him a name which is above every name: that at the name of Jesus every knee should bow, of things in heaven, and things in earth, and things under the earth; and that every tongue should confess that Jesus Christ is Lord, to the glory of God the Father" (Phil. 2:9–11). Amounting to something on your own is a futile project. Its danger lies in the fact that to do so is to grasp for glory which only God can bestow.

12

Yielding to Glory: The Call of God (On Heaven's Terms)

Genesis 12:1–3

Sin, like a malignant virus, entered the bloodstream of men, and when it reached epidemic proportions, God sent the flood across the earth, destroying every living creature except Noah and his family. Although Noah made a fresh beginning, the virus was still present. We witnessed its outbreak in the building of the great ziggurat at Babel. Again God stepped in, and this time he scattered men across the face of the earth, diversifying their languages. Following this the light of God grew gradually dimmer until men began to worship the sun or the moon or handmade idols. Sin had so blinded their minds that the inner compulsion to worship God was mutilated. Herein is the source of the manifold religions across the face of the earth even today. God said, "I have nourished and brought up children, and they have rebelled against me" (Isa. 1:2).

In the midst of inconsequential names listed in Genesis 11 there is one which is destined to be great. This is the account of God's beginning the third time to make something out of man. He chose a man named Abram, who lived in the heart of early civilization. In Ur, the capital city of the Chaldeans, wherein was the great temple to the moon god as well as countless other idolatrous temples, God spoke to the heart of a man who was ready to listen. Among all the forgotten millions of his time, Abram alone stands recognizable as a figure worthy of remembrance.

What was the significance of this man's life? Certainly it was not military or legislative or literary. Rather it was religious. To make such a statement is to bring an affront to the great areas to which most people search for significance, but nevertheless it remains so; a man's relationship to God determines his significance. What makes a man something? It is the call of God. Now to ask whether or not God calls or speaks to men is not even debatable. Multitudes throughout the annals of history affirm that such is true, and the greatest men of the ages maintain that it was God's call that made them so.

A Call to Faith

The call of God is a call to faith. Faith is synonymous with commitment. Therefore God's call is a call to the commitment of life itself. Day by day Abram heard in his soul the voice of God saying, "Get thee out of thy country, and from thy kindred, and from thy father's house, unto a land that I will shew thee." It was quite evident to Abram that to believe was to pack up and move. The voice was heard only by Abram, and yet, within his own soul it was a resounding, reverberating, ever-present cry. All about him were those who outwardly seemed to be content to bow down before the heavenly bodies and sacrifice the handmade idol—sacrifices which even included the burning of sons and daughters. But in the midst of all this Abram heard a voice. It was the voice of God.

There is something eternally edifying about a man who believes with all his soul that God has some purpose for him in this world and who thereby places himself at God's disposal. There is something refreshing about a person who is no longer bound by the expectations of his friends, or prevailing customs, of the prospect of profit and advancement, but who chooses rather to listen to the highest voice of all—the voice of God. While in the seminary it was my privilege to meet many men who were there studying because of the call of God. Many of them had left lucrative positions promising all kinds of earthly security and had packed up to follow the voice of

God. Now preachers are not the only ones who have a place in life. God has a place for every Christian to fill and a destiny for every Christian to live out. However there is always a certain amount of packing up and rearranging when a man proposes to believe God.

We are not to suppose that Abram was selected because he was perfect. He was not even perfect after his great faith commitment. In Genesis 17 he is skeptical about God's promise of a son because he is already old of age. In Genesis 12 Abram tells Pharaoh his wife is his sister lest Pharaoh desire his wife and take Abram's life to have her. He lied. Yet, the important thing to notice is that Abram is a man who is willing to turn his face toward God. He is willing to try his best to be what God wants him to be. A man preaching to convicts once said, "What with polygamy and slavery and occasional lying and deception, even the patriarchs, if they were living today, might have been in the penitentiary. But God, he said, regards a man's times and circumstances and his opportunity or lack of opportunity for full knowledge." [1] God has a place for every person to fill if he will but pack up and follow.

Real faith takes on the characteristics of an adventure. It may be a lonely one, for as Kipling wrote, "The race is run by one and one and never by two and two." [2] The venture of living faith must always proceed without rational security to back it up. Living faith does not demand a detailed diagram of every step which must be taken. But it does avoid the pitfall of a certain centipede:

> The centipede was happy quite
> Until the toad in fun
> Said, "Pray, which leg goes after which?"
> That worked her mind to such a pitch,
> She lay distracted in a ditch,
> Considering how to run. [3]

"Now faith means that we are confident of what we hope for, convinced of what we do not see" (Heb. 11:1, Moffatt). Faith is sometimes spoken of as an anchor, which it is, but we never see the full meaning of faith until we see it in terms of the hoisted sail filled with wind. Faith, then, is not the ship in the harbor but the ship putting out to sea.

Faith is selective. Faith is pinpointed. The faith spoken of here is faith in God. We are not speaking of the kind of eclecticism of the Hollywood star who said, "I believe in everything a little bit." The person who has faith in everything has no real living faith in anything—certainly not in God. Faith in God keeps believing when the door is bolted and shut. Faith believes that God is sufficient for any tragedy or any hardship. When famine takes Abram to Egypt, he is turned back to barren Canaan. The doors of Egypt's granary slammed shut before him. Yet in faith he goes back to the land of barrenness and his commitment is vindicated, because it is in the land of barrenness where he founds a great nation. In the granaries of Egypt he would have been lost among the people whom he could never have influenced.

Now we come to an important question: What have you risked in your life of faith? Have you ventured anything because of your faith in God which you would not have ventured even if you lived as a pagan? Suppose the impossible happened and God's promises all failed. Would you have lost anything in the process? If Christ were suddenly declared insolvent and incapable of fulfilling your hopes, would you find that you had ventured so much on his promise that you yourself are involved in his bankruptcy? In other words, if in nothing you have become poorer in order that you might have reward in heaven, then you have made no investment and run no risk. This means that if you have any faith at all it is terribly small.

Barnabas sold his Cyprus property (Acts 4:36–37) because

he believed heaven was his and in that kind of context his tiny parcel of land was a small thing indeed. To Barnabas his property became useful only so far as he could make use of it for God. Paul gave up his prospects of advancement in his own nation where he would certainly have become a famous leader. Paul risked everything for his faith, and if the word of God proved to be untrue, he would be a 100 percent loser, and, "of all men, most miserable." Now if you have made sacrifices you will know it and can name them. This is not to indulge in self-pity but it is to avoid self-deception.

A Call to Obedience

God's call always involves obedience which is another one of those lonely roads. It often means bursting out of a cocoon woven about us by the society of our times. Obedience is a costly experience and involves a great deal of risk. It means a willingness to put all your eggs in one basket—something the world warns you not to do. Abram was seventy-five years old when he left Haran, but his heart was still young in that it yearned to follow God's will. God's call knows no age limit. An elderly man once said, "According to the calendar I am an oldish man, but a few days ago I played baseball with some boys and I made a two-base hit. When I got to second, my breath was on first, but my heart was on third." [4]

The matter of obedience is contrasted in the lives of Cain and Abram. Cain chose not to obey God and thus every day of his life took him further from any destiny that could bring him fulfilment. Cain chose to travel about the earth as his own boss, living under the curse of God. Cain chose a life that was to bring him neither peace nor rest. In contrast, Abram chose the disciplined obedient life—within the framework of God's will and within the canopy of God's favor. Abram chose to travel through this world, not as a fugitive, but as a pilgrim.

A Call to Separation

Do not suppose that you can respond to the inner voice of God's calling and continue business as usual. God's call requires a definite separation. To begin with, one must separate himself from the world's standard if he is to propose to live according to God's. God can make little out of your life unless you are willing to live a separated life. "Wherefore come out from among them, and be ye separate, saith the Lord, and touch not the unclean thing; and I will receive you, and will be a Father unto you, and ye shall be my sons and daughters, saith the Lord Almighty" (2 Cor. 6:17).

One cannot propose to live for God and remain a part of the noncommittal Fifth Amendment crowd. The multitudes are willing to be saved by the cross of Christ, but they are not willing to take up Christ's cross and follow him. They desire to go to heaven but are not particularly interested in living a heavenly kind of life. They desire God but prefer godlessness. They don't want to be counted among the evil Philistines; yet, they are not willing to take their stand with the congregation of God. The call of God is a call to decision about this matter.

The call to separation is basically a call to decide whether or not one wants the world's approval or God's. To put it in rather archaic form, it is a matter of who you want to be "beholden to." In Genesis 14, Abram rescues his nephew Lot from the marauding kings and in the process captures certain goods worth a great deal of money. The king of Sodom offers these goods to Abram, but Abram chooses to decline the offer saying, "Lest thou shouldest say, I have made Abram rich" (v. 23). One needs to be on guard lest worldly powers ever be able to say, "I have made you popular" or "I have made you rich." If your popularity and success cannot be attributed to your Christian life and character, then beware of it.

Basically then, the call to separation is spiritual rather than geographical. It may be that God's calling for you is to stay put just where you are, among old friends, where you are to lead a wholly new life, abstaining from every appearance of evil (1 Thess. 5:22). This may bring violent opposition and severe criticism. You may be accused of fanaticism, but be sure of one thing: God's call cannot be lived out without some changes on your part.

A Call to Rich Rewards

Multitudinous are the rewards that come to any person who yields to the calling of God. Not least among these is strength for the trials which life holds. Abram found that answering God's call did not eliminate the trials but made them possible to be borne. Abram was childless for many years in spite of God's promise that there would be from his lineage a great nation. Abram was promised a land which was occupied by ungodly Amorites all the days of his life. Famine was prevalent throughout the lifetime of Abram and often caused him hardship. Yet Abram had the assurance of the promise which was finally voiced by the apostle Paul: "There hath no temptation taken you but such as is common to man: but God is faithful, who will not suffer you to be tempted above that ye are able; but will with the temptation also make a way to escape, that ye may be able to bear it" (1 Cor. 10:13). As G. Campbell Morgan has observed, "The nearer to heaven, the steeper the mountains." Yet one could go on to say that the steeper the mountains, the greater the presence of God. God's promise in Genesis 12:3, "I will bless them that bless thee, and curse him that curseth thee," is another way of saying that when a man proposes to do God's work, anything that confronts him must confront God also.

In the life of Abram we see that faith is rewarded with all those things that rebellion sought after but failed to seize. Abram's time was a great deal like our own—a time when men are on the move and striving to make a name and a place for themselves. Again and again in the early chapters of Genesis we see the sinful greed of men as they seek to make their own name, their own blessings, and their own nations. All of these efforts come to the same gloomy end apart from God. Yet, in Genesis 12, God gives by faith all of these things: a name, a nation, and blessings.

Life then is much like a relay race. We don't know how long we will have to run, but we do know that sooner or later our time will have ended and we shall have to hand on whatever there is of permanency to our children. One of the great rewards of yielding to the call of God is to be able to share this same faith with your own children and your own family, so that when life is over you may hand to your child the scroll of life.

Why then do you fear the voice of God and his calling? No man was ever commanded to do anything that was not for his own advantage. Sin is always a mistake and God's will is always the way of greatest blessing and accomplishment. The apostle Paul was so certain of this that he could say, "I reckon [I have totalled up all the columns] that the sufferings of this present time are not worthy to be compared with the glory which shall be revealed in us" (Rom. 8:18).

How does God present his call to your heart? God's call comes through Christ. You answer and surrender to God through a faith commitment to Jesus Christ. God chose to speak in a final way to all men by becoming flesh and living among us. Kierkegaard uses a simple story to illustrate God's revelation of himself in Christ. The story involves a king who secretly loves a simple rustic maiden. His problem was how to tell her of his love. If he went to her as king, she would be so overpowered by his sheer majesty that she would be won by fear instead of love. If he first made her a princess, it would ruin her rustic beauty which made him love her. The only way then to reveal his intentions and win her was for him to give up his majesty and go to her as a common man, and win her not as king but as commoner. This is something of God's way of telling man his love for him and his plans for him. God could reveal himself in splendor and majesty and overawe every one of us. But he chose rather to come as a man and to reveal his love and purpose for us in that fashion.

God is not your enemy from whom you must flee in order to live in freedom. He is rather your only hope. He is the only one whose love can deliver you from your chains that you may have freedom. He calls all men to come to him for salvation, and beyond that he has a special calling for every life. Some are to be preachers and missionaries, while others are to fill particular places of service as laymen. The question is: What is he wanting of you? The world says, "Seeing is believing." Don't believe it for a moment. If you wait until you can see all the way ahead you will never believe. The Bible reverses this and says, "Believing is seeing." In other words, a man first commits himself, and then, one step at a time, sight is given to him to show the way. Jesus said it like this in John 7:17, "If any man will do his will, he shall know of the doctrine, whether it be of God, or whether I speak of myself." You can answer God's call any time you are willing to do his will. You can't grasp glory. You can only yield to it.

13

Living by Faith

Matthew 8:26

The prophet Habakkuk admonishes his contemporaries to live by faith (2:4). The apostle Paul reaffirms this same directive as he says, "The just shall live by faith" (Rom. 1:17; Gal. 3:11). Jesus declares to his disciples that his followers are to live the life of faith. Yet it is very easy for one to lose sight of just what it means to live by faith. In Matthew 6:30 we hear Jesus say, "If God so clothe the grass of the field, which today is, and to-morrow is cast into the oven, shall he not much more clothe you, O ye of little faith?" When Peter began to sink amidst the waves we read, "Immediately Jesus stretched forth his hand, and caught him, and said unto him, O thou of little faith, wherefore didst thou doubt?" (Matt. 14:31). During the last week of his ministry, Jesus cursed a barren fig tree. The next day Jesus and his disciples passed the same way: "Peter calling to remembrance saith unto him, Master, behold, the fig tree which thou cursedst is withered away. And Jesus answering saith unto them, Have faith in God" (Mark 11:21–22). In Luke 18:8 we read, "Nevertheless when the Son of man cometh, shall he find faith on the earth?" (Jesus had spoken of a poor widow asking a judge to avenge her, and went on to say that God would avenge his elect who cry unto him day and night. Are the elect willing to live by faith in God to set things right?) All of these passages indicate the importance of living by faith. What does it then mean to live by faith?

Inadequate Approach

Not a call to conversion.—The context of Matthew 8:26 is that of a violent storm that descended on Jesus and his disciples while in a boat on the Sea of Galilee. Though a small body of water (only thirteen miles long and eight miles wide), the Sea of Galilee is noted for its sudden, turbulent storms. It is bordered on the west by mountains with many valleys and gullies. A cold west wind can arise suddenly and come sweeping down on the calm lake, lying 680 feet below sea level, and turn the placid waters into foaming whitecaps. In the experience of the storm the disciples are not questioning their commitment to Christ, and so we come to understand that what Jesus is saying cannot be interpreted to mean that to put faith in him is to live by faith. These men were following the Lord. They were in the boat with him. They had forsaken occupations and security to be with him. Yet we find these very men being admonished with regard to their faith.

Not running to God frantically.—There are many who think the life of faith means that each time a problem arises one frantically runs to God like a small child in hysterics and that this indicates the greatness of faith which one has put in God. Yet this does not seem to be what Jesus wants because the disciples do exactly this—crying for salvation from the storm, they run to the Saviour and roughly awaken him. Though some might call this living by faith, Jesus did not.

Not the idea that faith delivers from all harm or peril.—There are those who say that unless you are delivered from all problems or harm or sickness or peril that your faith is not what it ought to be. There are various miracle workers who say if you have a disease you are not living by faith. The disciples come running to Jesus and in effect say, "Does it not matter to you that we are drowning?" Oftentimes Christians want to ask God this question, "Doesn't it matter to you that

I'm in trouble?" They ask God this because they have the concept that faith should except them from difficulty and harm. Yet as you read the New Testament you find this is not the case. The apostle James was killed early by King Herod. Simon Peter, next in line to be put to death, was miraculously delivered from prison the night before his execution.

Hübmaier, the great Anabaptist preacher, was cruelly put to death. The great Polycarp was burned alive for his faith.

Scott, a devoted missionary to India, followed a wild heathen to his tribe and was immediately seized and spears were pressed against him. He closed his eyes, raised his violin, and expecting any moment to die, began playing and singing, "All Hail the Power of Jesus' Name." When he had finished, he was surprised when he opened his eyes to find the spears lying on the ground and tears in the eyes of those heathen savages. He spent two years preaching the gospel among them.[1] On the other hand, a few years ago in South America, five missionaries were cruelly murdered by a tribe with whom they sought to work.

Ira Sankey, traveling on a river boat, was asked to sing "Saviour, Like a Shepherd Lead Us." When he had finished, a man asked him if he had been on picket duty on a bright moonlight night in 1862. It turned out that the questioner had been about to pull the trigger and kill Sankey when Sankey began singing that song: "We are Thine; do Thou befriend us, Be the guardian of our way." The soldier had not been able to pull the trigger and thus Sankey had been miraculously saved.[2]

Yet history records that there were literally thousands of Christians who went to death in the Roman arena, singing the great hymns, and their singing did not stop the savage teeth of the lions who gnawed and clawed out their life.

All of this merely serves to illustrate the fact that living by faith does not necessarily mean one will be delivered from peril or even from death. So Jesus was not saying that the disciples would have been delivered from the storm if their faith had been great enough.

Biblical Approach

Trust God in the storms.—Living by faith is trusting in God's presence and providence. This is not to be equated with faith and trust in blind providence as such. It is solely from its object that faith derives any value. Only faith in God can be equated with living by faith. We, like the disciples, face sudden storms. When the sun is shining, the storm may be but moments away. There are many storms of life. There is the storm brought on by the bleak wind of sorrow. An old story is told of a gardener who had a favorite flower which meant a lot to him. One day he found it gone. Amid much distress and accusation, the master appeared and said, "Hush, I plucked it for myself." [3] There are the storms of temptations brought on by the hot blasts of passion. Robert Louis Stevenson once said, "You know Caledonian Railway Station in Edinburgh? One cold bleak morning I met Satan there." [4] There are the storms of doubt which sometimes rush in about the foundation of one's life.

Trust God, even if the ship sinks.—In trying to come to some understanding of what Jesus meant when he said, "How is it that ye have no faith?" one comes to see that he was actually saying, "Have faith in God even if the ship sinks." In Daniel 3:17 we hear the three Hebrew men answer the wicked king by saying, "If it be so, our God whom we serve is able to deliver us from the burning fiery furnace, and he will deliver us out of thine hand, O king. But if not, be it known unto thee, O king, that we will not serve thy gods, nor worship the golden image which thou hast set up." This is the kind of faith Jesus speaks of when he says we are to live by faith. We have faith that God can deliver, and still trust him if he does not.

Paul, knowing that his ship of life was sinking, said, "I am now ready to be offered, and the time of my departure is at hand. I have fought a good fight, I have finished my course, I have kept the faith" (2 Tim. 4:6–7). Someone has illustrated this kind of faith by comparing a thermostat with a thermometer. If in the same room there is a thermometer and a thermostat, this difference is easily noticed. When the room temperature drops, the thermometer does nothing but drop with it. The thermostat is a far different instrument. Immediately it sends a message to the furnace, "We need more heat." And when the room is warmed sufficiently, it calls to the furnace to shut off. People are much the same way. Some are thermometers and some are thermostats. The thermometers merely record the social pressure or private anxiety and accommodate themselves to them. The persons who live by faith are not molded by society nor by personal anxieties. Regardless of the risk, they remain firm in their convictions. Their faith in God is not a form, nor is their belief in truth and righteousness a mere profession. Their faith is a force for that which they believe right. It is the thermostats who will eventually control the world's pattern.[5]

Our Lord himself set the example as he prayed in the garden of Gethsemane. Anticipating his own crucifixion, he said, "Not my will, but thine be done." There is a difference in going with quiet trust to the Lord, and in running, screaming to him and demanding a miracle every time trials arise.

Living by faith means that we trust God's wisdom for our life even if it means the ending of our life. Clarence Macartney tells of an old minister friend who had had sorrow upon sorrow. He had gone blind; his child was crippled; his wife had died; and then his promising son in college died. Macartney said, "All I could say to him was that the Lord must love him more than most of us, because it is written, 'Whom the Lord loveth he chasteneth.'"[6]

Jeremy Taylor once said, "We are safe at sea: safer in the

storm God sends us than when we are befriended by the world. God's storms blow us to the port of repentance and faith." Thus Jesus would say to us, "Have faith in God, if the ship sinks, if the growth is cancerous, if the heart attack is fatal." I think this says something to us in the predicament in which we find ourselves in our troubled world. We live under an atomic cloud and realize that in such a world accidents can happen. One example gives us a hint of what can conceivably happen. "On November 25, 1959, at 4:52 A.M., a green light went out on a panel at the Strategic Air Command near Omaha, Nebraska. Within 12½ minutes at about 100 bases scattered over the world, 750 planes loaded with H-bombs taxied out to runways ready to go. They did not take off. Their commanders discovered that the light had gone out due to an overheated motor." [7] There is no need to exaggerate the danger; we know that no system of precaution can take danger out of our world. Yet, in the midst of these fearsome possibilities, the Christian is to trust God even if atomic war comes.

Not only are we to trust God in the face of such predicaments, but I believe we are to live optimistically in our trust toward him. There are those who have become nothing more than evangelists of doom. The greatest arousement of some of these evangelists of doom seems to be found in the words of Richard II, "For God's sake let us sit upon the ground and tell sad stories of the death of kings."

We must remember that he who has the power to command wind and waves can also cast out the forces of Satan. We must remember that the same power that can forgive the stain of sin in our lives has the power to raise the dead. This is the One in whom we can put our trust even if the ship sinks.

We are concerned with adding years to our life and appreciate so much the work of science which has done just this. In 1900 the average age was 47.3 years, while in 1962 it was 70 years. The promise is that by 1990 the average life span will be

81 years, and by the year 2050 the life expectancy will be 103. While it is good to add years to our life, living by faith will add life to our years and will make those years fuller and more meaningful.[8]

Though all men have faith, of sorts, there is no substitute for Christian faith. What catapults a man out of his faith of sorts religion, this religion of eminence, into Christianity is conviction of sin. When this has been faced and Christ has been accepted, then faith in blind providence, which is faith compassed about by fear, becomes living faith in Jesus Christ.

In the play *Joan of Lorraine,* Joan of Arc says to Bishop Cauchon: "Every man gives his life for what he believes. Every woman gives her life for what she believes. Sometimes people believe in little or nothing, nevertheless they give up their lives to that little or nothing. One life is all we have, and we live it as we believe in living it, and then it's gone. But to surrender what you are, and live without belief—that's more terrible than dying—more terrible than dying young." [9]

Since we do in effect give our life for what we believe, how tragic to give that life for empty belief when one can have living faith. Living by faith is the power to breathe easy even in the face of destruction. In the novel *Doctor Zhivago,* one of the characters says, "History as we know it began with Christ. . . . It was not until after the coming of Christ that time and man could breathe freely. It was not until after Him that men began to live toward the future. Man does not die in the ditch like a dog—but at home in history, while the work toward the conquest of death is in full swing; he dies sharing in this work." [10]

Yes, faith in Jesus Christ has allowed the world to breathe easy. It permits a consistent Christian life in the face of any tragedy or any storm. It does not deliver from all trouble, but it helps one to accept the will of God, to put himself within the framework of God's power, and to breathe easy.

14

The Last Look

2 Timothy 4:6–8

Someday we will stand on earth's brow, gaze upon our last sunset, and, as others have done, make the journey into another dimension that transcends time and mortality. The records of history are filled with so-called "last words" uttered by those who knew the last sunset had come. Some are full of despair. Voltaire said, "I am abandoned by God and man: I shall go to hell!" Edward Gibbon said, "All is dark and doubtful." Queen Elizabeth, dying as the ruler of a kingdom on which the sun never set, cried out in anguish, "Millions of money for an inch of time."

But the last words of some are inspiring. George Washington said, "Doctor, I am dying, but I am not afraid to die." John Wesley said, "The best of all, God is with us." Dwight L. Moody exclaimed, "This is glorious! Earth is receding, heaven opening. God is calling me!"

When one knowingly takes his last look at life, his words give a penetrating illumination into the deep currents of his life. Paul's valedictory address is climaxed by 2 Timothy 4:6–8 as he shares with us his last look.

The Vantage Point: Death's Door

Paul pauses on the threshold of the door marked death and turns to look back down the long road of life. It has been a life of sacrifice and hardship. Now he comes to the ultimate sacrifice: "I am now ready to be offered." The Romans had a custom of pouring out a cup of wine after each meal as a

109

libation to the gods. Paul indicates he is ready for life itself to be poured out as a sacrifice to God. The time has come for the living sacrifice (Rom. 12:1) to step from this earth into the hands of the Heavenly Father. There is no trace of tremor or anguish. Paul does not use the word "death." Some refuse to use it because of the dread it brings to their hearts—because it speaks of a coffin and a grave. Paul does not use it because death has a new tone. It is as gentle and welcome as falling asleep (1 Thess. 4:13). Thus he chooses to speak of death: "The time of my departure is at hand." The word translated "departure" was used of the unyoking of an animal from its plow, of the loosing of fetters, of the taking down of a tent, of the lifting of an anchor as a ship prepares to sail from the harbor. At last the time of the greatest journey of all has arrived. He senses a final fulness to the inspired truth he had written years before: "For none of us liveth to himself, and no man dieth to himself. For whether we live, we live unto the Lord; and whether we die, we die unto the Lord: whether we live therefore, or die, we are the Lord's" (Rom. 14:7–8).

Maclaren eloquently says: "The only life that bears being looked back upon is a life of Christian devotion and effort. It shows fairer when seen in the strange cross lights that come when we stand on the boundary of two worlds, with the white radiance of eternity beginning to master the vulgar oil lamps of earth, than when seen by these alone. All others have their shabbiness and selfishness disclosed then." [1]

The Focus: All of Life

In moments when death seems certain it is said that one sees all of life flashed before him. In such a glimpse the trivia give way to what has been the basis of all the major emphases and decisions. In such a look, Paul can say, "I have fought a good fight, I have finished my course, I have kept the faith." What a wonderful testimony to be able to come to that moment with no regrets or excuses. Erasmus, the Reformation scholar, when life was almost gone, said, "I am a veteran, and have earned my discharge, and must leave the fighting to younger men."

In a world beset by dropouts, Paul challenges us to complete the course ordained for us by God. It requires "a good fight." Literally Paul says, "I have struggled a good struggle." There is no way to "keep the faith" apart from a constant, agonizing struggle. By "the faith" Paul means the total gospel message, involving his personal commitment to Christ and the propagation of the body of truth found in Christ. He has never lost hope or confidence in Christ and his gospel.

As Paul's night of earth comes, he rejoices that he has triumphed over his greatest fear expressed years before: "But I keep under my body, and bring it into subjection: lest that by any means, when I have preached to others, I myself should be a castaway" (1 Cor. 9:27). Paul never feared for his soul's salvation for he knew whom he had believed (2 Tim. 1:12). What he did fear was the possibility that he might do something in a moment of weakness that would disqualify him for his task under God. His greatest fear was that he might become unusable and have to be set on the shelf.

Just prior to his death, columnist William F. Kirk looked back on life and wrote:

> The doctor knows what his trained eyes see,
> And he says it is the last of the ninth for me;
> One more swing while the clouds loom dark,
> And then I must leave this noisy park.

> 'Twas a glorious game from the opening bell,
> Good plays, bad plays and thrills pell-mell;
> The speed of it burned my years away,
> But I thank my God that He let me play! [2]

No one's life is without its hardships and disappointments. Certainly Paul's wasn't: "We are troubled on every side, yet

not distressed; we are perplexed, but not in despair; persecuted, but not forsaken; cast down, but not destroyed; always
bearing about in the body the dying of the Lord Jesus, that
the life also of Jesus might be made manifest in our body" (2
Cor. 4:8–10.)

Paul does not look back on a life in which everything was a
glorious victory. There were times of crisis, like that of his first
trial, when he had to say, "No man stood with me, but all men
forsook me" (2 Tim. 4:16). "Alexander the coppersmith did
me much evil" (v. 14). "Demas hath forsaken me, having loved
this present world" (v. 10). Demas is one of the dropouts who
failed to bring to completion God's purpose for his life. The
Scripture passage records his spiritual decline. He is "fellow-
labourer" (Philemon 24), then just "Demas" (Col. 4:14), then
the one who "has forsaken me." Perhaps he just got tired and
decided someone else could carry all the load. There is a
spiritual middle age spread more injurious than the physical
one.[3] His convictions were not deep enough to resist the
constant allurement and seductions of the world's glitter. The
last we hear of him, he has moved to Thessalonica, like many
modern church members who have moved to new localities
and chosen to remain anonymous, spiritually. It is difficult to
cling to the riches of Christ when you are clutching the ashes
of this present world.

Yet one thing relegates the disappointments to their proper
place—"Notwithstanding the Lord stood with me, and
strengthened me" (2 Tim. 4:17). Even if all others desert you,
God is by your side. Though no man stood with him at his first
trial, Paul looks forward to the mighty multitudes in heaven
where "Eye hath not seen, nor ear heard, neither have entered
into the heart of man, the things which God hath prepared for
them that love him" (1 Cor. 2:9). As life's eventide begins to
ebb, Paul lifts his eyes beyond the human horizon and affirms,
"Henceforth there is laid up for me a crown of righteousness,

which the Lord, the righteous judge, shall give me at that day: and not to me only, but unto all them also that love his appearing" (2 Tim. 4:8). In the past he "has fought." In the present he is "ready to be offered." In the future there is "a crown."

The Admonition: Be a Witness

The charge delivered to Timothy is a challenge to us as well. In it are solemn thoughts about the place of the gospel, and its urgency, in our lives. We, like Timothy, will one day face those we have witnessed to, and those we have failed to witness to, concerning their need of Christ. Heed this awesome admonition: "I charge thee therefore before God, and the Lord Jesus Christ, who shall judge the quick and the dead at his appearing and his kingdom; preach the word; be instant in season, out of season" (2 Tim. 4:1-2).

The gospel is never out of season. It is always appropriate. Its message alone prepares a man for death and judgment. Therefore each of us must "do the work of an evangelist" (v. 5). Men pass swiftly from the boundary of opportunity where life eternal may be grasped by faith in Christ. In the last dim light of our earthly pilgrimage, it will be the cross of Christ that stands silhouetted against the backdrop of all human affairs. All else will lie in the darkness of its eternal shadow.

The events of life are like the operation of an adding machine. The time will come when the "total" key is pressed. In a second, all of life will be calculated and the evaluation will stand for eternity. In between time, let us stand alongside the apostle Paul and envision our last look which we shall someday take before stepping into God's tomorrow.

15

Victorious Certainties

Romans 8:38–39

"I have become absolutely convinced that neither death nor life, neither messenger of Heaven nor monarch of earth, neither what happens today nor what may happen tomorrow, neither a power from on high nor a power from below, nor anything else in God's whole world has any power to separate us from the love of God in Christ Jesus our Lord!" (Rom. 8:38–39, Phillips).

There is an apocryphal story about a man who believed himself to be dead. His psychiatrist told him to use every idle moment for two weeks to repeat, "Dead men don't bleed." The man did so, and when the two weeks were up the psychiatrist took him into the inner office and had him once again say aloud, "Dead men don't bleed." Then the psychiatrist pricked the man's finger with a pin causing a few drops of blood to appear. "Now what do you say?" asked the psychiatrist. To the dismay of the psychiatrist, the troubled man exclaimed, "Dead men do bleed!"

This story reminds us that sometimes we have a hard time convincing ourselves of what we know to be true. There comes a time when one must stop verbalizing faith and start living by it. Nothing can take the place of action. There is no biblical faith apart from action and commitment.

Recently I sat and listened to the anxieties of a troubled woman who was expressing a desire to begin to live for the Lord. During the course of the conversation she declared that, among other things, she was going to stop smoking. The room was already clouded by her chain smoking but she lit another cigarette, inhaled, and blew smoke in my face as she repeated her determination to give up the habit. What she needed to do was to put her feelings into action. Her problem was that down deep inside she wasn't certain she wanted to give up smoking, or start living for the Lord either, for that matter.

The apostle Paul's testimony was that he had "become absolutely convinced" that the Christian way was the only way which offered real life and hope. This book has been written to encourage each reader to become equally convinced. The purpose has been to set forth a practical framework in which the fragments of life may be fitted together. Just as the student must sometime graduate and begin to be a responsible part of his world, so the Christian comes to the time when he must go beyond the philosophical, rise above the dialectical of his own problems and anxieties, and begin to exhibit the faith he professes. Before leaving you to this adventurous journey, I want to lay before you the Bible's format for facing the future via the life of Paul.

"I am sure" can be dangerous words. Spoken prematurely they can bring on what someone has called the "sound sleep of a decided opinion." During the yellow fever epidemic in New Orleans over a century ago some of the "authorities" were sure that the percussion of a brass band would disturb the atmosphere and effect a cure. However the ill were disturbed more than the yellow fever. Alfred North Whitehead said, "When I was a young man, I was taught science and mathematics by brilliant men. . . . Since the turn of the century I have lived to see every one of the basic assumptions of both set aside. . . . And yet, in the face of that the discoverers of the new hypotheses in science are declaring 'now at last we have certitude.'" [1] The cave man was "sure" that peace would prevail if he could make clubs so powerful that his enemies would be afraid to attack him.

Yet it is possible to be sure about spiritual matters based on the promises of God. God's promises have been proven in every generation by people of faith who have been willing to put them to the test in real life. The Bible invites you to do the same and experience the joy of complete assurance. There are certain victorious certainties that you don't have to live without as you face the future.

No Pessimism

There is much in the world about us to cause pessimism. Nature is subject to unpredictable rampages. Disease stalks us. Men deceive us. Death awaits us. "What shall we then say to these things?" (Rom. 8:31). This question is not only found in the Bible, it is in the heart of every man. Shall we lament our sad lot? Shall we curse our bad luck?

One morning a couple on vacation were nearing the town in which I lived when the man suffered a massive heart attack while driving. He slumped over the steering wheel, causing the car to careen off the road and overturn. The newly-made widow obtained a room in a motel operated by a member of my church who called me on the phone. Amidst her sobs, the woman told me how her own life had been spared because of a "religious" charm she wore on her necklace. Almost in a state of shock, she recounted the morning's events and how she had almost forgotten to wear the charm, having had to unpack her suitcase at the last minute to find it. This woman pathetically illustrates the multitudes who place all their hopes on superstitious luck.

Let others grow bitter in the face of Lady Luck's fickle disillusionment, but not the Christian. His answer is simple, "If God be for us, who can be against us?" (Rom. 8:31). This does not mean the Christian is never pessimistic. He is always pessimistic with regard to man's ability to build and plan, apart from God. He is certainly pessimistic about any utopian ideas propounded by idealistic groups, for the Bible tells us there will always be "wars and rumors of wars." But the Christian is never ultimately pessimistic, for he awaits the coming of another age, another world, where complete and final victory will be his through Christ.

Therefore the Christian never denies that he has much against him. He merely affirms that God's presence outweighs any adversity.

The grounds for such an affirmation are found in Romans 8:29-30: "For whom he did foreknow, he also did predestinate to be conformed to the image of his Son, that he might be the firstborn among many brethren. Moreover whom he did predestinate, them he also called: and whom he called, them he also justified: and whom he justified, them he also glorified."

The theme of this passage is the doctrine of election, or predestination. Notice that this is a doctrine for Christians. It has no relevance for a non-Christian. There is no purpose in discussing the biblical teaching on tithing, or the Lord's Supper, with a non-Christian for such doctrines are meaningful only to the believer. So the doctrine of election is relevant only to the believer. It is given to bring assurance to the Christian's heart—assurance that God worked in the past to bring him to salvation, and will continue to work in the future to complete his salvation. The doctrine of election grows out of the Christian's own experience as in retrospect he realizes that all through his life God was guiding him toward salvation.

Predestination is based on God's foreknowledge. God knows the ending from the beginning. This foreknowledge does not cause men to accept or reject Christ. Predestination is a doctrine of assurance that the Christian's destination is to be one of eternal glory. This is where predestination leads. God has predestined the Christian "to be conformed to the image of his Son." Romans 8:30 is a golden chain in which every link is

forged and held together by God: God calls, declares righteous those who respond, and proceeds to lead them through
the ravines and gullies of a sin-scarred earth to an eternal
glory. The glorification which is yet to come is spoken of in
the past tense since its culmination is certain: "Them he also
glorified." Denney says this is the most daring tense in the
New Testament.

Predestination enters history by means of God's calling:
"Whom he did predestinate, them he also called." This has to
do with God effectively calling men through Christ. (Remember, God's calling is always through Christ). It is like a man
saying to his guests, "You are my invited guests." Of course
there were many that were invited but didn't come. What the
host means is, "You are the guests who accepted my invitation." This is what the Bible says: "For ye see your calling,
brethren, how that not many wise men after the flesh, not
many mighty, not many noble, are called" (1 Cor. 1:26).

We are not to conclude from this that God's Spirit does not
work in the hearts of the wise and noble. The meaning is that
many of those who are wellborn see no need of being born
again spiritually. They decline God's calling.

Someone has said that when you approach heaven's gate
you will see above it the words, "Whosoever will may come,"
and once inside you will see above it the words, "Chosen from
the foundation of the world."

Let me emphasize again that this doctrine of predestination
is given to bring assurance to the Christian. It is to have no
bearing on our efforts to reach the unsaved masses. We must
ever announce to them the invitation of God, "Whosoever will
may come."

Romans 8:32 is the clincher in the Christian argument
against pessimism: "He that spared not his own Son, but
delivered him up for us all, how shall he not with him also
freely give us all things?"

No Condemnation

Although the Middle Ages is usually characterized as a time when people felt condemned and were obsessed by feelings of guilt, men of every age have certain similar anxieties. Actually such anxieties are a man's only hope for they are meant to lead him to see his need of forgiveness. Any man who is honest with himself realizes he has sinned. However, a part of the good news of the gospel is that faith in Christ leads the soul into a realm of sonship where there will never be condemnation. The heavy burden of guilt is lifted.

Nevertheless, the fact that no one achieves sinless perfection causes many Christians to continue to live in fear of the final judgment. The Bible deals with this subject by means of leading questions. The first question is: "Who shall lay any thing to the charge of God's elect?" (Rom. 8:33). In other words, who can stand in the day of judgment and file charges? Can enemies or persons we have offended do this? The worldly crowd would like to try, as one has written:

Indeed, many of the so-called "world's people" live on the faults, real or imagined, of God's professed children—a most miserable diet! —and some of them by their talk and actions would seem to think that if they could take an imperfect minister and a few delinquent church members with them to the bar of God it would go all right with them in the judgment. No doubt God's true people are faulty enough. Indeed, their own hearts and consciences are their swiftest and loudest accusers. But if God will justify the sincerely penitent believer as being found in Christ, all accusations of the ungodly will be in vain.[2]

Who can bring any charge against a Christian on the day of judgment? God alone can. But remember, it is the God who has already declared his children not guilty (Rom. 8:33).

The second question is: "Who is he that condemneth?" The answer is: "It is Christ that died, yea rather, that is risen again, who is even at the right hand of God, who also maketh intercession for us" (Rom. 8:34). In other words, the only one who has the power to condemn is Christ, who has made our salvation possible through his death and resurrection. He is the Christ who cares and helps. Dr. William Ashmore's tract shows a Chinaman in a pit. Confucius looks into the pit and says, "If you had done as I told you, you would never have gotten in." Buddha looks into the pit and says: "If you were up here, I would show you what to do." Both Buddha and Confucius walk on. Then Christ leaps down into the pit and helps the poor Chinaman out.[3] The final judge is the one who has rescued us from the pit. As Christians, we have no cause for anxiety concerning a final condemnation.

No Separation

Of all the biblical metaphors depicting sin, perhaps none is more relevant to our age than that of estrangement. We know a great deal about estrangement. Millions of displaced persons roam our earth. The breakup of homes is more evidence of estrangement. Great separators are abroad in the world. There are the pressures of a complex society that tear us from our desires and leave us feeling like a sucked orange. With every war comes separation of loved ones as men march away from brides and cradles, never to return.

Therefore we understand perfectly when the Bible tells us that sin separates us from God and his purpose for our lives: "Your iniquities have separated between you and your God, and your sins have hid his face from you, that he will not hear" (Isa. 59:2).

However it is a different matter after conversion. We experience a union with Christ which nothing can sever. The Bible has this to say: "Who shall separate us from the love of Christ? shall tribulation, or distress, or persecution, or famine, or nakedness, or peril, or sword? As it is written, For thy sake we are killed all the day long; we are accounted as sheep for the slaughter. Nay, in all these things we are more than conquerors through him that loved us. For I am persuaded, that neither death, nor life, nor angels, nor principalities, nor powers, nor things present, nor things to come, nor height, nor depth, nor any other creature, shall be able to separate us from the love of God, which is in Christ Jesus our Lord" (Rom. 8:35–39).

There are two major categories of separators. The first might be labeled "daily circumstances."

Included here are the pressures of life, the struggle for food and clothing, the unseen dangers of sickness and accidents, the heat of persecution, and the peril of war. The Christian is not exempt from any of these. In fact, there are times when it will seem that he has more than his share, and he will feel a kindred spirit to the words of the apostle: "I think that God hath set forth us the apostles last, as it were appointed to death: for we are made a spectacle unto the world, and to angels, and to men" (1 Cor. 4:9).

The second category is composed of even more formidable separators. Death heads the list. J. S. Whale speaks of the difference between the death of men and of animals:

Only man is genuinely concerned with tomorrow, and the irrevocable yesterday, and the pathos of his mortality. Only a Macbeth can brood over time as the way to dusty death. Death is the common doom, admittedly, of this Macbeth and this little beaver; of elephant and chimpanzee and the most intelligent sheep-dog that ever was. But Macbeth is aware of it as they can never be. They die; he *has* to die. There is a difference of dimension between dying and having to die; and in this very difference—in this distinctively human awareness of a temporality which expresses itself supremely in death—man already stands above temporality and death. He is aware of time because he belongs to eternity.[4]

The Christian is not only aware of being a part of eternity, he has chosen his eternity. Death cannot separate him from this destined eternity but rather will transport him to it.

There is a touching scene in the movie about the *Titanic* when all the men are left on board the sinking ship while the women and children row away in the lifeboats. Suddenly the brass band begins to play and the men's voices float through the inky stillness singing, "Nearer, My God, to Thee." For the Christian, death ceases to be a separator and instead brings him face to face with the Heavenly Father.

Strangely enough, life is listed as a possible separator. But perhaps this is not so strange after all. Life, with all its distractions, its interests, its seductions, is often deceptive enough to lead weak men away from all hope. The death of the unbeliever is but the finalization of a whole way of life.

Next come angels, principalities, and powers. These are the unseen spiritual forces concerning which the apostle says: "We wrestle not against flesh and blood, but against principalities, against powers, against the rulers of the darkness of this world, against spiritual wickedness in high places" (Eph. 6:12).

"Things present" lumps together all earthly eventualities that this present age can muster. "Things to come" looks forward to the coming age. Neither will separate the Christian from God's love and purpose.

"Height" and "depth" (*hupsoma* and *bathos*) were current astrological terms. Many ancient people believed their destiny was determined by the position of the stars. These words indicated the highest and lowest orb of a star.[5] The Bible is saying there is no need to fear the stars (people who buy horoscopes need to hear this promise) or any other superstitious signs.

At the end of the list is the phrase, "nor any other creature." This is not equal to et cetera. Literally it reads "nor any other creation." This is especially meaningful to our space-oriented age. Suppose some new world, some new creation, is discovered. Such a discovery will have no bearing on our faith or our relationship to God. The cross will never be eclipsed. The purpose of God for us stands firm. We can join with the apostle in saying, "I am persuaded."

Christ is no fair-weather friend who forsakes us when the going is rough. Through him we have a religion of surpluses. The world has had its conquerors in the personages of men like Alexander and Augustus. Yet we are "more than conquerors through him that loved us" (Rom. 8:37).

We don't know all that is to happen, but we know how it all will end. Someone has remarked that in the filming of *Quo Vadis*, Deborah Kerr wasn't afraid when the lions rushed at her in the Colosseum, because she had read the script to the end and knew she would be rescued. The Bible is our script. We know the ending.

The Christian life is a marvelous journey. It has about it the awesome and the glorious. It is the paradoxical way of the cross and the crown. Let us live it joyfully and hopefully. Let us live it daringly and soberly. Armed with the assurance of God's presence, let us go forward into whatever the future has with a doxology on our lips: "Now unto him that is able to keep you from falling, and to present you faultless before the presence of his glory with exceeding joy, to the only wise God our Saviour, be glory and majesty, dominion and power, both now and ever. Amen" (Jude 24–25).

Notes

Chapter 1

1. W. H. Auden, *Age of Anxiety* (New York: Random House, 1947), p. 134. Used by permission, Random House, Inc.
2. Although some translations of Romans 5:1 read, "We have peace," the best manuscripts read, "Let us enjoy peace with God." For a full discussion, see A. T. Robertson, *Word Pictures in the New Testament* (Nashville: Broadman Press, 1931), IV, 355.
3. Findley Edge, *A Quest for Vitality in Religion* (Nashville: Broadman Press, 1963), p. 80.
4. O. Hobart Mowrer, *The Crisis in Psychiatry and Religion* (Princeton: D. Van Nostrand Co., 1961), pp. 26, 37, 54, 56–57.
5. *Ibid.*, p. 51.
6. *Ibid.*, p. 78.

Chapter 2

1. E. Stanley Jones, *Victory Through Surrender* (New York: Abingdon Press, 1966), pp. 116–17.

Chapter 3

1. Translation mine.
2. F. Godet, *Commentary on the Epistle to the Romans*, "Classic Commentary Library" (Grand Rapids: Zondervan Publishing House, 1956), p. 317.
3. From the *New Testament in Modern English* © J. B. Phillips 1958. Used with permission of The Macmillan Company.
4. Halford E. Luccock, *Preaching Values in the Epistles of Paul* (New York: Harper & Bros., 1959), I, 58.

Chapter 4

1. George A. Buttrick, *God, Pain, and Evil* (New York: Abingdon Press, 1966), p. 44.

2. Clarence E. Macartney, *Macartney's Illustrations* (New York: Abingdon Press, 1945), p. 350.

3. Ella Wheeler Wilcox, "One Ship Drives East," in *One Thousand Quotable Poems*, ed. Thomas Clark and Esther Gillespie (New York: Harper & Row, 1937), I, 148–49. Reprinted by permission, First Church of Christ Scientist, Maywood, Ill.

4. C. S. Lewis, *The Problem of Pain* (New York: The Macmillan Co., 1962), p. 96.

5. Quote from Edmund Burke in Buttrick, *op. cit.*, p. 178.

6. Macartney, *op. cit.*, p. 351.

7. Lewis, *op. cit.*, p. 93.

8. *Ibid.*, p. 95.

Chapter 5

1. *Christianity Today*, November 8, 1963, p. 54.

Chapter 6

1. Louise Tarkington, "The Land of Beginning Again," Clark and Gillespie, *op. cit.*, II, 70.

Chapter 7

1. Harold Bosley, *Sermons on the Psalms* (N. Y.: Harper & Bros., 1956), p. 103.

2. Eddie Lieberman, *The Whirlwinds of Life* (Greenville, S. C.: published by Eddie Lieberman, 1957), pp. 18–19.

Chapter 8

1. Luccock, *op. cit.*, 172.

2. *Ibid.*, 180.

3. Raymond Davis, *Fire on the Mountains* (Grand Rapids: Zondervan Publishing House, 1966).

Chapter 9

1. Robertson, *op. cit.*, VI, 17.

Chapter 10

1. Paul S. Rees, *The Adequate Man* (Westwood, N. J.: Fleming H. Revell Co., 1959), pp. 113–14.

2. *Ibid.*, p. 121.

3. Luccock, *op. cit.*, II, 207.

4. Reinhold Niebuhr, *The Nature and Destiny of Man* (New York: Charles Scribner's Sons, 1941), I, 182.

5. Paul Tillich, *The Courage to Be* (New Haven: Yale University Press, 1952), pp. 35–36.

6. Luccock, *op. cit.*, p. 208.

7. *Ibid.*

8. Rees, p. 10.

9. *Pulpit Digest* (March, 1960), XL, 58–59.

10. William Barclay, *The Letters to Philippians, Colossians, and Thessalonians* (Edinburgh: The Saint Andrew Press, 1959), p. 104.

11. Robertson, *op. cit.*, 463.

Chapter 11

1. Helmut Thielicke, *How the World Began* (Philadelphia: Muhlenberg Press, 1961), p. 278.

2. Richard W. Solberg, *God and Caesar in East Germany* (New York: The Macmillan Co., 1961), p. 242.

3. Edwin Markham, "Man-Making," in *Masterpieces of Religious Verse*, ed. J. D. Morrison (New York: Harper & Bros., 1948), p. 419. Reprinted by permission, Harper and Row.

4. J. S. Whale, *Victor and Victim* (Cambridge: University Press, 1960), pp. 113–14.

5. Ralph L. Murray, *From the Beginning* (Nashville: Broadman Press, 1964), p. 114.

6. *Ibid.*, p. 117.

Chapter 12

1. George Buttrick (ed.), *The Interpreter's Bible* (New York: Abingdon Press, 1952), I., 567.

2. "Tomlinson."

3. Mrs. Edward Craster, quoted in John Bartlett, *Familiar Quotations* (Boston: Little, Brown & Co., 1955), p. 942.

4. Buttrick, *op. cit.*, 569.

Chapter 13

1. Walter B. Knight, *Master Book of New Illustrations* (Grand Rapids: Wm. B. Eerdman's Publishing Co., 1956), p. 632.

2. *Ibid.*, p. 629.

3. William Barclay, *The Gospel of Mark* (Edinburgh: The Saint Andrew Press, 1958), p. 114.

4. ———, *The Gospel of Luke,* p. 105.

5. Harleigh Rosenberger, "Take a Lesson from Life," *Sunshine Magazine,* February, 1966, p. 6.

6. Macartney, *op. cit.,* p. 14.

7. Roger L. Shinn, *Tangled World* (New York: Charles Scribner's Sons, 1965), pp. 116–17.

8. Russell J. Fornwalt, "Are You Adding Life to Your Years?" *Sunshine Magazine,* February, 1966, p. 5.

9. Maxwell Anderson, "Joan of Lorraine," in *The Best Plays of 1946–47,* ed. Burns Mantle (New York: Dodd, Mead & Co., 1947), p. 60. Copyright 1947, Maxwell Anderson. All rights reserved. Reprinted by permission, Anderson House.

10. Boris Pasternak, *Doctor Zhivago* (New York: Pantheon Books, Inc., 1958), p. 10. Used by permission of Random House, Inc.

Chapter 14

1. Alexander Maclaren, *Expositions of Holy Scriptures* (Grand Rapids: Wm. B. Eerdman's Pub. Co., 1944), XV, 109.

2. Knight, *op. cit.,* p. 159.

3. William Barclay, *The Letters to Timothy, Titus, and Philemon* (Philadelphia: The Westminster Press, 1960), pp. 244–45.

Chapter 15

1. Luccock, *op. cit.,* 66–67.

2. Alvah Hovey (ed.), *Acts and Romans* in "An American Commentary on the New Testament" (Philadelphia: The American Baptist Publication Society, 1882), p. 211.

3. A. H. Strong, *Systematic Theology* (Philadelphia: The Judson Press, 1907), p. 178.

4. Whale, *op. cit.,* p. 150.

5. William Barclay, *The Letter to the Romans* (Edinburgh: The Saint Andrew Press, 1955), p. 124.

Acknowledgments

I would like to acknowledge my indebtedness to the memberships of the churches I have served as pastor who graciously allowed me the opportunity of continuing my education while a student and who later allowed me the time to write this book. A special note of appreciation is due Mrs. Kathryn Stephenson for her tireless efforts during the typing of the manuscript. And last, but not least, I want to express appreciation to my wife, Ann; my son Mark; and my daughter, Debra, without whose love and encouragement this work could not have been written.

The King James translation of the Scriptures is the one quoted unless otherwise specified.